theatrebook

**a compact guide
to staging your play or musical**

Allan T. Duffin

published by

duffin creative

los angeles

Published in the USA by
Duffin Creative
11684 Ventura Blvd #205
Studio City, CA 91604
Visit us on the Web at duffincreative.com

Cover photograph by Kimberlee Kessler Design. Used with permission.

ISBN-10: 0692380396
ISBN-13: 978-0692380390

Printed in the United States of America

Table of Contents

Introduction

As a freelance writer I've had the privilege of writing about the theatre and the amazing people who bring works of art to life in front of an audience. I've collected many of those writings in this book in the hope that the information will be of use to those who work in the theatre—as well as those who are interested in what happens behind the scenes.

Whether you're a theatre manager, staff member, crewmember, performer, drama department head, high school or college instructor, acting teacher, agent or manager, or curious theatregoer, you'll find something in this book that'll interest you. From business practices to stagecraft to special effects, there's a little something for everyone in here.

I hope you enjoy the book. If you have any questions, please feel free to contact me through my website at www.aduffin.com.

—*Allan T. Duffin*

Web-Savvy Marketing:
Navigating your way in the digital age

Web sites. Podcasts. Blogs. Social networking. Video downloads. Smartphones and iPods. RSS and iTunes. Some of these Internet-based tools have existed for years, while others recently came online and are growing by leaps and bounds. Many are part of what's collectively known as "Web 2.0," the next generation of the Internet, where interaction, sharing and collaboration are the watchwords. It's enough to make anyone's head spin, but for marketing to a new generation that grew up with computers practically from the womb, these Web tools are rapidly becoming an essential part of marketing in the theatre industry.

How can theatres reach the Web-savvy younger generation? "Like many theaters around the country," says Susie Falk, director of marketing for California Shakespeare Theater in Berkeley, Calif., "we were concerned about the national decline in subscriptions." To attack the problem, Cal Shakes launched its "New Generations" program, targeted to individuals in the 18-to-35 age group. The program blends low-tech marketing tools—discounted tickets, pre- and post-show parties—with high-tech methods like Web-based message boards, blogs, podcasts and video presentations.

Podcasting Your Way to Fame

By contrast, some theatres are taking a more gradual approach to their 21st-Century marketing strategies. At the Circle Theatre in Grand Rapids, Mich., a small community venue that celebrates its 54th birthday this year, Managing Director Joe Dulin and his staff formed the Circle E-Team, a group of volunteer patrons who use the Internet to spread the word about the theatre's latest efforts. The staff then added "behind-the-scenes" podcasts to accompany each of their productions.

These podcasts are audio files that are downloadable from the theatre's Web site or from Apple's iTunes online store. Each program features directors and actors discussing their roles and careers. Production costs for the podcasts are minimal, since all that's really required are a microphone and computer to record, edit and upload the audio. Meanwhile, RSS (Really Simple Syndication) allows theatres to notify their patrons — via computer software known as an RSS reader, a 21st-Century version of the teletype machine — if a podcast or Web site has been updated. In this way, theatres can stay in constant communication with their audiences.

At the Nashville Opera in Nashville, Tenn., Artistic Director John Hoomes and the marketing staff headed by Reed Hummell added podcasting to their advertising lineup. The resulting monthly program, "In Studio with John Hoomes," features lively discussions between the artistic director and visiting principal singers appearing in the Nashville Opera's productions.

Impressed with the initial podcasts, Executive Director Carol Penterman asked her staff to pioneer a synchronized director's commentary for the upcoming production of "Romeo and Juliet." This podcast, downloadable to an iPod or other MP3 player, is "a test of technology," says Hoomes. "We'll synch commentary with the live performance," similar to the directors' commentaries available as a special feature on popular DVDs. "People are interested in how the show is put together, how it's cast, and what the dramatic intent is," explains Hoomes. As with the Circle Theatre's podcasts, the Nashville Opera keeps its production simple, with three members of the staff acting as audio engineer, producer and computer operator, respectively.

Social networking

If you've created a Facebook or MySpace page or uploaded family photos to Flickr.com lately, you've ventured into the incredible world of social networking on the Internet. Theatre organizations are also taking advantage of the wide-ranging memberships of these Web sites to promote their latest productions.

At Oklahoma City University, the popular OCU Summer Music Program for high school students is entering its 10th year. Dan Meagher, director of marketing, notes that aggressive marketing to a niche demographic—high school music students and their parents—has resulted in impressive feedback from potential participants. OCU created a MySpace group which now boasts over 600 high school students as members. "While some might look at MySpace as lower-tech marketing," notes Meagher, "it gives us instant access to students all over the nation and the world."

Across the Web at Flickr.com, a photo sharing site, Infernal Bridegroom Productions maintains an extensive archive of snapshots from all of its events. "It's incredibly useful," says Lisa Haymes, managing director of the Houston-based theatre company. "Audiences like to see photos as soon as they are uploaded, and peruse the galleries of older productions. And when reporters ask for images, I can send them to this site and have them pick out exactly the ones that they want."

Infernal Bridegroom Productions also launched a highly successful blog — essentially a diary open to everyone on the Internet — to publicize its production of the late playwright Eugene Ionesco's "The Killing Game," a collection of scenes about plague and death. The blog, hosted on Blogger.com, is a good example of how a simple Internet query on the Google or Yahoo search engines can lead Web surfers to unexpected information. As Haymes explains, "People found the blog through our company Web site or by searching for information about Eugene Ionesco, the Black Death, the plague or, of course, killing games."

Another marketing tool for Haymes' organization is the use of free video clips to advertise its productions. Haymes recently posted a seven-minute excerpt of Suzan-Lori Parks' "365 Days/365 Plays" on the popular video-sharing site YouTube, where anyone in the world can view it. However, this approach has its drawbacks: "Theater is difficult to reproduce in video," says Haymes, "so we are still experimenting with the best way to use YouTube for our purposes."

No More Paper Tickets?

Still getting used to e-tickets? The major airlines introduced Internet e-ticketing in the mid-1990s, providing what was advertised as a simpler, streamlined method of buying and printing travel tickets. Today's phenomenon of convenience is "mobile ticketing," in which a digitized bar code is displayed on the screen of the patron's cell phone. The theatre staff then uses another handheld device, perhaps a phone of their own, to scan the bar code from the patron's phone. In essence, the cell phone itself acts as a ticket.

Mobiqa, headquartered in Edinburgh, Scotland, is one of a growing number of technology firms that offer "mobile ticketing" for theatres. "We're involved in the creation, delivery and redemption of barcoded tickets to mobile phones in over 30 countries," says Iain McCready, Mobiqa's CEO. McCready notes that Mobiqa issued a world-record 20,000 mobi-tickets for the O2 Wireless Festival, a music extravaganza that took place in the cities of London and Leeds in the United Kingdom. Mobiqa is developing the mobi-ticket one step further: its "mobi pass" system, which displays a text message with a barcode and double-checks the patron's identity with a photo ID, can save on distribution and operational costs for the venue while saving time for the patron, who no longer needs to stand in ticket lines.

Tickets via cell phone: the theatre scans the bar code from your phone's display screen. *(Photo courtesy of Mobiqa)*

Choose Your Cost

Taking advantage of the Web to promote your theatre doesn't have to be a costly proposition. Internet marketing offers a rich menu of options, some of which cost very little. To produce the Circle Theatre's podcasts, Joe Dulin and his team needed little more than computer equipment and a relatively soundproof room. Meanwhile, the Nashville Opera's podcast with director's commentary cost less than $1,000 in computer and audio equipment. "And," adds John Hoomes, "word-of-mouth advertising is free!"

At California Shakespeare Theater, the staff has funded its New Generations venture through a two-year, $64,000 grant from the Doris Duke and The Andrew W. Mellon Foundations. New York-based Theatre Communications Group administers the grant. Cal Shakes is already planning for its next phase by applying for another round of foundation grants and seeking corporate sponsorship to underwrite its discounted-ticket program.

New Marketing, New Customers

How can theatres measure the effectiveness of their Web-based marketing campaigns? Sometimes the results are difficult to gauge. It's relatively simple to track the number of visitors to a Web address or examine how many times a podcast was downloaded. But these statistics, available from your hosting service, can't track all of the demographic information. Having site visitors provide their e-mail addresses or some personal information can help.

Sometimes the best feedback is anecdotal. At the Nashville Opera, John Hoomes has received strong positive response to his organization's efforts at podcasting. "Our patrons are very intrigued," notes Hoomes, who says that the new technology is transcending generations. "During rehearsals a woman in her 70s came up to me," he recalls. "She said that she was coming back for her third or fourth show, and she was bringing her iPod! She had never downloaded a podcast before, so we showed her how."

Reaching the patron of tomorrow will become more involved as computer technology continues its upward trend, says Reed Hummell of the Nashville Opera. "It's critical that we are receptive to a changing marketplace, and are prepared to adapt. My children will grow up with cellular phones, iPods, text messaging, TiVo, laptops ... and the like. They will expect to be able to incorporate these types of technologies into everything they do ... and we have to be ready."

Multimedia Magic:
How theatres are embracing multimedia on stage

At Henry Ford Community College in Dearborn, Mich., a spell-bound audience wearing 3-D glasses leans forward in their seats as glittering lights zoom overhead. Onstage, actors garbed in futuristic spacesuits are bathed in orange and red fire as an electrical storm rages around them. The production, which premiered in 2003, was a science-fiction staging of Shakespeare's "The Tempest." But this version of the well-known play sported a fresh twist: the cast meshed with riveting three-dimensional multimedia, creating an aural and visual experience that blended classic stagecraft with cutting-edge digital technology.

Dr. George Popovich, director of the Virtual Theatricality Lab at the college, began his adventures in multimedia in 1995, when the college's technology investment fund awarded him a grant to explore the use of computer-assisted teaching aids. During the next five years, Popovich investigated the latest in computer hardware and software, animation and 3-D stereoscopic projection. His science-fiction take on "The Tempest" hit the stage soon thereafter, followed by a production of Caryl Churchill's "The Skriker" in 2006.

"Rather than produce a freak 'em out in your face' style production," noted Popovich during the run of "The Tempest," "we wanted as many traditional theatre audience members as possible to view our show. The point was to demonstrate how digital techniques could be applied to traditional theatre and not just the obvious choices such as performance art and other stylistic experiments."

The advantages of digital technology include "improved quality of audio and video, increased flexibility, and simplification of technical systems at the operator level," says Jim Tetlow, owner and principal consultant of Nautilus Entertainment Design, Inc., in La Jolla, Calif. The company helps create lighting, audio, video and special effects systems for theatres and other entertainment facilities like cruise ships, Las Vegas hotels, and even the Senate and House chambers in the Capitol Building in Washington, D.C.

With digital lighting equipment like the DL.3 and Barco DML-1200, for example, "users can change their set design on the fly, thereby reducing hardware costs and labor time," says Debi Moen, marketing communications specialist for High End Systems. "Panoramic set-ups are also achieved quickly, thereby eliminating or reducing the need for actual structural sets."

Audio, lighting and video

One of the most difficult things about working with multimedia is that the technology encompasses such a huge variety of equipment. From front- and rear-projection screens to drapery and audio systems, the sheer number of "multimedia" elements can seem overwhelming. Although it might feel like digital technology has been around for a long time, it's worth noting that Virtual Theatricality Lab's version of "The Tempest"—the second production in the world to use 3-D stereoscopic projection and real-time virtual-reality scenery—premiered within the last decade. For theatres that are experimenting with multimedia or are simply exploring the possibilities, a variety of consultants and equipment vendors stand ready to help.

Jim Tetlow separates the multimedia world into four areas: audio, lighting, video and integrated control. When designing audio systems, says Tetlow, "We have been specifying all-digital audio consoles for most new theatres, using predominantly products manufactured by Yamaha including the PM1D and the PM5D." Digital consoles offer control over a large number of audio channels in a compact space, says Tetlow. In addition, the consoles contain most of the audio processing needs—equalization, limiting and effects, for example—that used to be done by separate pieces of equipment.

In the lighting arena, "while we are still dependent on more traditional theatrical lighting fixtures," notes Tetlow, "the use of LEDs (light-emitting diodes) is becoming more prevalent with new products coming to market on a continual basis." Tetlow points to LED products manufactured by Color Kinetics, Pulsar, and SGM of Italy.

Not just for theatres on land: Nautilus Entertainment Design consulted on the creation of the main showroom on the *Splendor*, a new 3,006-passenger cruise ship operated by Carnival Cruise Lines. *(Photo courtesy of Nautilus Entertainment Design)*

Vendors such as Rose Brand and High End Systems supply gear and technical support to theatres around the world. Secaucus, N.J.-based Rose Brand handles multimedia sales through its Dynamic Scenery/Technical Services department. "We deal with LEDs and fiber optic drapes," among other items, says Product Manager Jeff Brown. Rose Brand serves as a distributor for products like the Soft-LED drapery from Mainlight, the ShowLED line of lighting effects, and additional products manufactured by Acclaim.

The newfangled video technology you have at home is becoming more prevalent in the theatre, where Tetlow notes a dramatic increase in the use of plasma and LCD video displays from manufacturers like NEC, Samsung and Sharp. Playback of video for productions is typically handled by a media server such as Rose Brand's Panorama or High End Systems' Axon.

Video displays can also be used in the house and lobby to run previews and other advertising. "Most of the theatres we're looking at these days are embracing the lobby video monitor," says Randy Willis, supervisory consultant and manager of media systems at McKay Conant Hoover, Inc., a consultancy with locations in Westlake Village, Calif., and Scottsdale, Ariz. During a show, says Willis, the large flat-panel displays in the lobby can show video of the performance. That way, "folks who come late and don't want to interrupt the performance don't have to miss anything happening onstage while they wait to take their seats," he explains.

Integrated Control

Having a solid collection of multimedia equipment can be helpful, but theatres need a piece of computer hardware to automatically coordinate everything onstage. An integrated control system like those made by AMX and Crestron allows a production to control various multimedia elements through an "Internet Protocol," or IP, network. IP is a communications protocol that provides a speedy method for hardware and software to talk to each other. "The user interface is typically a small color LCD touch screen that is used as the operator interface for lighting, audio, video, rigging and other effects," explains Tetlow.

From the home page of the integrated control system an operator can select a different page for each subordinate system and then control many of the system options. For example, on the audio page, an operator can select an audio device such as a microphone or CD player and then adjust the volume of each device. On the lighting page, recorded presets can be recalled for both the house lighting and theatrical lighting systems. On the rigging page, the operator controls curtains and projection screens. "If a show has been pre-programmed, then the entire production can be started and stopped from this simple-to-operate control panel," says Tetlow.

The bottom line: budget and capability

Digital audio and video might be snazzy, but the technology can also be quite expensive. When shopping around for new equipment, "make sure you know what you want and what you want to do," urges Popovich. "Always have the company come to your venue and demonstrate the equipment."

Popovich's multimedia facility is a rarity in that he, his staff and students purchased and installed all of their equipment—everything from $40,000 in Barco projectors, to $160,000 in Vicon motion-capture cameras, to a $1,500 Behringer MX 9000 sound mixer. But for most theatres, sitting down with a design consultant is critical in making the shift to multimedia, especially when budget is a key issue. Brown notes that renting a media server can cost $700 a week, while an outright purchase runs between $7,000 and $10,000 depending on what options are installed.

In Arizona, McKay Conant Hoover is currently consulting on a 1,500-seat theatre that has "just started to touch on the multimedia aspect of what they can do," says Willis. Among other possibilities being discussed, the theatre would like to be able to run a lightly staffed show with very little setup, and to use video presentations during dance performances. Willis is preparing information about product configurations that match the theatre's requirements.

Knowledge needed

Keyboards, touch screens and interactive graphics might make your new digital equipment seem simple to use, but the bells and whistles can be deceiving. "At the operator level," says Tetlow, "it provides a simpler interface for complex systems. However, at the set-up and maintenance level it can be more complicated and require a background in IP networking."

Brown notes that the Panorama media server was designed for the skilled theatre technician with little or no experience on such a piece of equipment. "We like to think that a skilled technician can be using Panorama in a day," he says. "Obviously, like all theatrical control equipment, the operator will become more skilled with more use." Furthermore, he says, the system can be installed by the theatre staff or by a technician supplied by the vendor. "We're happy to send out one of our technicians to install and train, if that's the client's desire," says Brown.

Why not stick with the tried-and-true?

If your theatre is happy with traditional methods of staging, is there any need to convert to digital multimedia at all? "In the big picture, I don't see the transition from analog to digital as an option, but rather a necessity," says Tetlow. "The question becomes, at what point do you change to digital systems, and how do you deal with it?" The best way to prepare, he adds, is to retrain existing theatre technicians and look carefully at the résumés of new or potential employees to see if they have the background to work with digital multimedia and networks.

Unfamiliarity shouldn't be a roadblock, says Willis. Theatres are becoming more comfortable with using multimedia technology in their day-to-day operations, as opposed to loading in video and audio equipment for a specific performance. "It's now part of the thread of their everyday production," he says.

"My advice is not to be scared of the new video technologies," notes Brown. Most of the best products are not difficult to understand and use—and they can change the nature of scenic and lighting design."

Safety First:
From trips and falls, to emergency preparedness and handling unruly patrons, is your theatre a safe haven or a disaster waiting to happen?

Tom Andrews recalls a Broadway production that was touring the United States a number of years ago. During lunchtime one day, a work light suddenly exploded, sending flames and molten glass across a nearby backdrop.

Thankfully, though, something brought this disaster-in-the-making to an abrupt halt: the backdrop was flame-retardant. "The drape burned in the area where it was exposed to the flame and molten glass," recalls Andrews, "but the fire didn't spread any further than that. If the drop hadn't been treated to withstand the flame, it would have caught fire, spread to other drops and burned the theater down."

For Andrews, this story hits close to home: he's the president of Turning Star, Inc., of Brooklyn, N.Y., which offers retardant products and services to a variety of clients, including major theatres across the country. Safety is his business. "People need to remember that 90 percent of fighting a fire is preventing it," says Andrews.

Whether due to electrical problems, malfunctioning props or pyrotechnics, chemical leaks, or simple mistakes, theatres are always at risk for accidents. A thorough safety program can save your theatre time, energy, and money in the long run.

Top safety concerns in the theatre

Recently a number of theatres wrestled with major safety issues during their productions. The new musical version of "Lord of the Rings" in London's West End was put on hold for safety tests when the mechanical stage swallowed part of an actor's costume, dragging him down and mangling his leg. In Aspen, Colo., an actor playing Brutus in a production of Shakespeare's "Julius Caesar" accidentally cut himself with a real knife during the murder of the title character. The Telfair Peet Theatre at Auburn University shut its doors for nearly two days after cast and crew stumbled over a toxic chemical spill near some mechanical equipment.

Operating a safe theatre means putting the well being of your staff and the audience first. The safety manual for theatre students at the University of Wisconsin Oshkosh offers a useful perspective on the subject: "A theatre space, especially the stage area, is essentially a large machine for producing plays. It contains many hazards, especially to those unfamiliar with the mechanical and physical aspects of a theatre." Avoiding those hazards—and preparing for potential accidents—is at the heart of every safety plan.

At the Old Creamery Theatre in Amana, Iowa, Producing Artistic Director David Kilpatrick heads the state's oldest professional theatre company in a 300-seat facility. As part of his safety preparations Kilpatrick also wrestles with a climate issue: the possibility of tornadoes. When necessary, "we move our audience into the area underneath the seating, where there are braces and supports, as it is the most secure point in the building," he explains. During a recent show the state issued a tornado warning just before curtain call, and Kilpatrick and his staff quickly ushered the audience to safety, with some of them squirreled away in the bathrooms.

"The audience should remain our biggest concern," says Bob Bertrand, general manager of Rose Brand in New York. Bertrand praises the state of today's safety awareness and enforcement, which have greatly decreased the risk to audiences in standard venues. However, he cautions that this type of vigilance extends to the staff as well: "Given the constant presence of the staff in venues beyond performance time and the temptation to relax safety procedures when the audience is absent, staff members are exposed to more opportunity to suffer injuries day in and day out," he says. These include "the same kind of concerns you'd find at any construction site," including items falling from overhead (lights, tools, and rigging) and misuse of ladders and scaffolds.

In the safety zone underneath the seating area of the Old Creamery Theatre in Amana, Iowa, are (left to right) Chris Priebe (concessions manager), Jerri Priebe (box office manager), Sean McCall (actor and associate artistic director), Deborah Kennedy (actress and company manager), David Kilpatrick (producing artistic director). *(Photo courtesy of The Old Creamery Theatre, Amana, Iowa)*

Getting Started

Where can you hunt for information with which to build a safety program? The federal Occupational Safety and Health Administration (OSHA) provides basic guidelines. In addition, creating a safety committee for your theatre not only allows for effective cross-communication among departments. "A committee should consist of representatives from all areas of a facility and should have at least one person from senior management," recommends Bertrand. "Each regularly scheduled meeting needs to start with a report and review of any incidents since the last meeting—including near-misses," he adds. "Each member is responsible to educate his or her co-workers in their respective area as well as solicit their safety concerns."

Creating an emergency plan for your theatre is another critical facet of any good safety program. According to Andrews, the plan should include fire prevention as well as emergency response procedures. "The production or theatre staff can devise a plan, and then ask the local fire marshal to review it with them," he says. For additional information, Bertrand recommends that supervisors review the National Fire Protection Association (NFPA) 101 Life Safety Code document, which prescribes safety regulations for buildings and other potential hazardous areas.

If writing a safety plan sounds daunting, don't worry: the document doesn't need to be long or complex, and you can ask other theatres for copies of their plans in order to get you started. The Victory Gardens Theater in Chicago, Ill., built a 23-page Emergency Action Plan that outlines procedures for responding to medical emergencies, gas leaks, bomb threats, malfunctioning elevators, suspicious mail and robberies. "Our first priority is always personal safety," says Jay Kelly, director of marketing and publication relations. "Our house manager acts as our emergency coordinator." During an emergency, the box office becomes a command post where the coordinator can manage the theatre's incident response and communicate with the rest of the staff.

Several pages of the Victory Gardens emergency plan are

dedicated to evacuation procedures which split the building into five zones and explain how to move the audience and staff out smoothly. According to Bob Bertrand, proper egress is critical, especially in nontraditional venues like clubs, community and small regional theatres, off-off Broadway, and "event environments" like haunted houses and murder mystery stagings. "These venues need clear and well-marked points of egress to be used in any type of emergency," he says.

Arming Yourself with the Right Gear and Training

Proper training and equipment will ensure that your staff knows what to do when the ball drops. For example, the Victory Gardens Theater stashes away the following items in its emergency kit: area maps, building maps and blueprints, a staff list with phone numbers, a list of emergency services and telephone numbers, phone lines, flashlights, bullhorns, first aid kits (with ice packs), and fire extinguishers. All of these items are strategically placed throughout the facility in locations like the main stage, administrative office and concession stand.

Theatre staffs need to be familiar with the fire safety equipment that's required by law—"fire extinguishers, fire alarm systems, sprinkler systems," says Bertrand, who consults with fire marshals across the country every day. In addition, Bertrand urges that stagehands familiarize themselves with any local requirements for stage scenery in addition to NFPA Code 701, which details the fire resistance of temporary decorations in public spaces. NFPA 705 provides a field test that can verify the flame-resistance of a fabric.

At Turning Star, Andrews urges theatres to store scenery and paint supplies carefully and properly; ensure that scenery, drapes and related soft goods, set dressing and costumes are appropriately flame retardant; and double-check that electrical and lighting systems are safe for use. During an emergency the theatre staff must coordinate smoothly with each other. "Chain of command and communication are key so that staff members do not take it upon themselves to make conflicting decisions and statements," he adds. Andrews recommends that theatre staff rehearse their fire emergency procedures, with volunteers playing the audience.

Chemicals and Other Hazards

Have you checked your shops lately? A quick inspection can prevent money-burning delays in your production schedule. When Auburn University closed its Telfair Peet Theatre due to a chemical spill, officials from the school's department of risk management and safety quickly ran an inspection and determined that the substance was mercury, which is extremely toxic when inhaled or absorbed through the skin. Fortunately the mysterious spill was tiny and posed little threat to the cast and crew, but because of the cleanup the production came to a standstill just two weeks before opening night.

A selection of flame-retardant chemicals (liquids and powders) available from Rose Brand for treating natural and synthetic fabrics, wood, paper, cardboard, foliage, paints and varnishes. The chemicals can be applied via spraying, painting, rolling or immersion treatments. *(Photo courtesy of Rose Brand)*

To prevent incidents like this one, it's critical that any chemicals present on the job are properly labeled and handled. If you need assistance, a number of organizations will inspect your facility for you. Monona Rossol is president and founder of Arts, Crafts and Theater Safety, Inc., a New York-based nonprofit corporation that provides health and safety services to arts organizations. As part of her menu of services, Rossol offers inspections to check compliance with OSHA standards regarding, among other things, chemical storage and disposal, personal and respiratory protection, proper ventilation, sanitation, and sources of toxic building materials such as lead paint and asbestos.

In addition, ACTS publishes over 60 data sheets on subjects like proper handling of ceramics and dyes and methods for detecting carbon monoxide. Data sheets like Rossol's are a useful supplement to the Material Safety Data Sheets (MSDS) required by federal law as part of a workplace Hazardous Communication Program. MSDS typically contain information about the safe use and hazards associated with a particular chemical. In addition to OSHA, the Environmental Protection Agency, state and local agencies also establish their own requirements, so be vigilant in navigating your way through the requirements for your theatre.

By integrating a safety program into your day-to-day operations, your staff will be ready whenever an emergency occurs. At the Old Creamery Theatre, David Kilpatrick has one basic rule for his staff: protect the audience. "Appear like we know what we are doing and the audience will feel safe," he says. "They are trusting us—so let's be worthy of that trust."

Tips for creating a safe theatre

Create a safety program for your theatre and put it in writing. Coordinate with government agencies and the local fire marshal to ensure that you've covered all the bases.

Make sure that your theatre is in compliance with local and state health and safety regulations. Start your research by checking with the Occupational Safety and Health Administration (OSHA).

Create emergency checklists for incidents related to evacuations, accidents, fires, chemical spills and weather, to name a few.

Conduct regular safety inspections of your facility. Contract with external agencies to bring in trained inspectors—they can catch things that you might have missed.

Designate someone on your staff as the health and safety monitor to oversee training and communication needs.

Brief safety issues to your staff on a regular basis. If you don't hold separate safety meetings, cover safety issues during your regular staff meetings.

Pay attention to the small things: proper egress with exits clearly marked, hazardous chemicals properly labeled, and combustible materials treated with flame retardant, for example.

Ensure that your insurance policy is up-to-date and provides the coverage you need.

Stock an emergency kit with items like flashlights, bullhorns, list of telephone numbers, first aid kits and fire extinguishers. Place the kit in an easy-to reach area.

Designate a staff member as the emergency coordinator—the person who will lead everyone during accidents and emergencies.

Thoroughly train your staff to handle emergency situations quickly and calmly. They're your first line of defense in protecting the audience and your theatre when the unexpected happens.

Safety: The potential costs of being unprepared

Bottle of flame-retardant spray for fabrics: $13.50

Rebuilding of theatre after backdrops catch fire and building burns down: $20 million

Roll of electrical tape: $5.00

Replacement of damaged equipment after an electrical fire: $150,000

Safety inspection conducted by independent firm: $750/day

Hospital costs for a cast or crewmember suffering a work-related injury: $10,300

Roll of non-slip tape: $50

Settlement in occupational injury lawsuit: $750,000

Safety training for theatre staff conducted by independent firm: $750/day

OSHA fine for inadequate safety procedures: $197,500

Amounts are examples only and do not apply to every situation. Sources: Rose Brand, Turning Star, Arts, Crafts & Theater Safety, Inc., Agency for Healthcare Research and Quality, OSHA.

**Sizing Up Your Seating:
With all of the built-in flexibility of seating
that is available today, are you as adaptable
as you could be finding more spaces and
places for your patrons to sit?**

Several years ago, when the Orange County Performing Arts
Center in Costa Mesa, Calif., needed to accommodate a variety
of seating configurations in its new Samueli Theatre, management relied upon experts in audience seating to give the venue
maximum flexibility. The resulting design allowed for 375 patrons
in stadium seats or a club/cabaret style with 320 people grouped
around tables of four, among other layouts.

One of the contractors involved in the project was StageRight
Corporation, based in Clare, Mich., which sells a range of seating
products for everything from small presentations to major event
staging. Whether your theatre seating is fixed or moveable, choosing the right vendor is critical. "Theatres should look for a supplier who will take the time to gain a better understanding of the

scope of the project," says Bill Gareiss, vice president of sales for StageRight.

Gareiss notes that other manufacturers he typically sees involved in flexible seating projects are the Wenger Corporation and Staging Concepts. Other available vendors include Comfor Tek Seating, Seating Concepts and Stage Technologies. To select the best fit for your theatre, "do your homework ahead of time to define the scope and uncover all the needs of the project," urges Gareiss. "Research two or three different manufacturers to seek the best fit for your theatre."

In addition, Gareiss recommends that theatre administrators include their staffs in the decision-making process: "The most successful projects include a team approach where the operations, programming and front office are all involved."

Maximum flexibility for your venue

Whether you're overhauling a fixed seating layout or figuring out how to utilize ramps, decks and risers in moveable configurations, it's important to balance a number of factors. "The challenge lies within selecting seating that will meet needs of space, capacity and quality versus the available budget," says Alex Tiscareno, spokesperson for San Diego-based Seating Concepts LLC.

Maximizing a theatre's seating configuration provides better sightlines to the stage, allows the greatest number of patrons to see your shows—and consequently increases your box office receipts. "As a producer, I want the maximum number of seats in there," says Jim Bumgardner, who oversees student theatre productions at Bergen Community College in Paramus, N.J. The college's Ender Hall Laboratory Theatre is a black box that seats anywhere from 80 to 125 people depending on the type of show. "Each time we put in a new set we redo the seating chart as quickly as possible," he adds.

Bumgardner keeps one eye on aesthetics and the other on maximizing the floor space in the theatre. "I always encourage my designers and tech staff to explore," he says. "Our black box is one of my favorites here because the various configurations allow designers to express themselves differently, and allow actors the intimacy that a black box can bring."

The Whitney Theater at Yale University in New Haven, Connecticut, used StageRight's ML1600 Risers. Seating capacity is 130 with portable seats.
(Photo courtesy of Stageright Corporation)

Products to make the most of your space

Let's say you're ready to sit down with a consultant or vendor. Before you do so, says Tiscareno, request references from those potential contractors. Ask for information about their past installation projects that are similar to your own. That way you get a sense of the contractor's capabilities and quality of service.

Then, "check with your local municipality to determine what current building, flammability and ADA (Americans with Disabilities Act) compliance codes will affect the quantity and seating scheme for the venue," says Tiscareno. In addition, closely examine the existing floor layout: is it flat, sloped, limited by fixtures or posts? When Preferred Seating LLC of Indianapolis, Ind., was hired to provide new seating for the auditorium at South Carolina State University in Orangeburg, S.C., "we installed 1100 seats on risers and also on a forced slope," recalls Director of Marketing Frank Sumner.

When preparing proposals for clients, Gareiss looks at "a plan view and elevation drawing of the performance space including dimensions of the room, exits and entrances, ceiling height, the shape and size and location of storage areas for portable equipment, and the location and size of the doorways and hallways, including any freight elevators that lead to and from the portable equipment storage areas." Other useful information: the theatre staff's ideas for types of configurations they need, type and size of seat to be used, and a goal for quantity of seat in each configuration. "Understanding all these scope issues will ensure that the best system of portable riser and storage equipment will be used for the project," explains Gareiss.

The use of moveable risers can improve sightlines for patrons and allow for multiple seating layouts for different types of performances. The Joan and Irwin Jacobs Center, a performance space at the La Jolla Playhouse in California, uses StageRight's ML1600 portable risers to seat audiences from two to 450 people. Transportability, storage capability and ease of use are crucial for a seating system, says Gareiss: "A good system will get used in many configurations because it is easy to set up and change from performance to performance."

Moveable seating should also be sturdy and quiet. Noisy equipment distracts the audience from what's happening onstage. A riser system that doesn't lock properly can sway back and forth—and possibly injure patrons if it fails to operate properly.

Comfort and sightlines: picking the right seat for your audience

For your specific venue you might perch folding chairs on risers or bolt permanent seats into the floor. Either way, be choosy when selecting the type of chair in which your patrons will reside during performances. "Ask for a sample of the product," says Tiscareno. "Test the seat and investigate if the comfort you feel today will still be present in the future after the venue has undergone a substantial amount of patron traffic." In addition, inquire if the sample chair will work with the theatre staff's criteria for quantities of seats in each of the planned floor configurations.

At Bergen Community College's black box theatre, Jim Bumgardner and his crews use individual seats for their audiences. "We found that individual chairs work better for us than connected ones," he notes. This flexibility comes in handy since the theatre has been configured as a proscenium stage, a thrust, three-quarter round and, at one point, a long narrow stage in the middle "with the audience on either side like a basketball court," says Bumgardner.

When investigating what seats are best for your venue, make sure that the product sample meets your expectations regarding style and aesthetics. Seating should feel comfortable and also mesh with your theatre's decor. When administrators at Michigan's Port Huron High School renovated their auditorium, they knew that the 650-seat venue would host both academic and community productions. Their final choice was Seating Concepts' BA 205 Performer Series, which provided a choice of fabrics and a plastic laminate or wood veneer back surface to match the auditorium's overall design scheme.

Tiscareno notes that the overall comfort of the chair is critical. Is it cushioned in such a way that will allow the patron to enjoy the performance instead of wondering why his or her back is hurting? Will a patron's knees clear the seat in front of him, or bump up against it? When Bumgardner plans out his seating configurations, "it's important to have comfortable padding with plenty of leg room," he says.

Also important, adds Tiscareno, are the manufacturer's warranty and post-installation technical support. "Some manufacturers provide only an industry-typical one-year warranty period," he explains, "or a warranty that appears to be generous" but features fine print explaining that certain parts of the warranty actually expire *during* the period of coverage.

Finally, order spare parts for future use. "It is quite a bit less expensive to order spare parts during the initial manufacturing of the seating product, than years later when the product is priced on an individual component basis," says Tiscareno. "This includes extra sewn fabric seat and back cushion covers."

Items like sloped floors and portable ramps—providing accessibility per the Americans with Disabilities Act—ensure that all patrons can comfortably attend your productions. Venues like the Warner Theatre in Washington, D.C., designate specific seating areas to accommodate patrons who are disabled or have other special needs. At the Warner Theatre, the front side orchestra section is reserved for patrons who are visually impaired or need clear line-of-sight to a sign language interpreter.

Installation, training and operation

"Most of the good manufacturers will include an on-site installation including a training period for the staff," says Gareiss. He adds that supervisors who take a hands-on approach to the process will ensure that once the supplier departs the job site, the entire theatre staff will be completely familiar with the equipment and how to use it properly and safely.

With seating charts viewable online these days, theatres benefit greatly from merging a new seating configuration with their box office ticketing software. Seating Concepts, for example, provides post-installation seating layout media for submittal to software vendors. In addition, says Tiscareno, "the company is pleased to answer any and all questions regarding the seating scheme for the owner's associated vendors."

The total number of seats is important in calculating royalty payments to the rights holders of each production, says Bumgardner. "I have to come up with a minimal number of seats," he explains. "If we can get a few more in, we can sell them at the last minute at the box office. It makes a difference when we pay royalties." More seats means a higher royalty payment —a percentage of gross ticket sales—but also a larger income at the box office.

No matter what the production—from an intimate black box performance to a gigantic stage show—a flexible seating system can make the most of the space you have. "The goal is to meet as many needs as possible," says Gareiss.

The Ups and Downs of Dimmers: How to get the best lighting control for your theatre

A gorgeous mix of light, color and shadow creates the kaleidoscope that brings a stage performance to life. "Besides the obvious need to provide visibility," says Jeffrey E. Salzberg, a lighting designer whose productions include dance, theatre, opera and puppetry, "lighting can direct focus, reinforce mood and theme, and furnish punctuation. It can create a universe—realistic or not—for the characters to inhabit."

Careful choices make all the difference, says James David Smith, president of the Canadian company RC4 Wireless in Etobicoke, Ontario. "Just as music is not turning on all the notes at the beginning of the show and turning them all off at the end," he says, "the fluid and dynamic art of lighting design demands control of the available lighting instruments. The lighting designer is the conductor, and the lights are his orchestra."

To that end, manufacturers and their vendors offer a rich variety of dimming systems to suit your theatre's needs. Dimming equipment ranges from the simplest packages for black boxes to complex arrangements for the largest venues. According to Salzberg, "dimming systems can range from small 'shoebox' dimmer packs that hang on the grid next to the fixture and cost less than $100 to large systems with several 192-dimmer racks costing tens of thousands of dollars each."

At Angstrom Lighting in Hollywood, Calif., Frans Klinkenberg and his staff install and rent customized systems for a variety of venues. "Dimmers can be small and plug into standard outlets or they can range from 12 to hundreds of dimmers," he says. "The dimmers themselves can have capacities ranging from 800 watts to 12,000 watts per dimmer." The most common dimmers, he adds, are 2400 watts per dimmer and come in 12, 24 or 48 dimmer racks.

Strand Lighting, a manufacturer in Cypress, Calif., offers two families of control consoles, the Light Palette and Palette. The company supplies everything from schools to large performing arts venues. Peter Rogers, vice president of marketing, stresses the importance of adaptability. As examples, he points to Strand's systems, which offer connectivity for conventional dimmers, the latest moving lights and even PowerPoint presentations.

What type of dimming equipment is best for your theatre? Shawn Priebe, sales and marketing director of Theatreworks in Hollister, Mo., recommends installation racks, located in a central area and wired to power strips, for the simplest type of plug-and-play system. For venues that lack enough electric power or space, dimmer packs are a good option: "Packs are fed power near the fixture location," he explains, "and the fixtures plug into the pack with no distribution system needed." Another option is the "stick" dimmer, which is similar to the pack but is elongated to fit above or below the lighting batten.

Manufacturers like Strand and ETC supply a variety of dimming equipment and control systems. ETC, or Electronic Theatre Controls, is based in Middleton, Wisc., and offers two families of dimming equipment for small and large venues. Priebe notes that smaller theatres might consider purchasing gear from companies like Lepracon or NSI. "Someone has to fill that niche market, and they do it very well," he says.

New and emerging technologies

Over the years, manufacturers have improved on existing technology, notes Priebe, by reducing lamp "singing" (hum), heat output and buildup, and power distribution, to name a few. "The most exciting new technology in dimmers is the LED fixture, which doesn't require dimmers," says Salzberg. LED equipment provides the designer with thousands of color options that are changeable from cue to cue.

Expanding on the current DMX technology, Remote Device Management (RDM) allows the designer to assign DMX channels automatically and receive status information from the various devices installed around the stage. While it's a bit complex for small productions, Smith says that RDM "can be fantastic for touring shows, rigs that set up and tear down frequently, and ever-changing configurations of equipment."

Ellen White, who handles marketing for ETC, notes that new SineWave technology, which virtually eliminates lamp noise or hum, is a bonus for acoustically sensitive venues with more generous budgets.

Using lighting control with maximum effect and minimum expense

To do it right the first time, rely on an experienced designer to target the right lighting requirements for your theatre, rather than basing decisions on what happened during previous productions. "Many times," says Priebe, "we've had customers call to tell us they want X-number of ellipsoidals and Y-number of moving lights and Z-number of par cans. Eventually it comes out that that is what the theatre manager had at his last venue."

ETC's Smart family of portable products provides standard phase-control dimming technology in a super-compact form. *(Photo courtesy of ETC)*

According to Klinkenberg, designers should create a "repertory light plot," a document containing lighting information for that specific venue. "The most complicated light plots are musicals with lots of dance numbers," he says. "If that can be specified into the venue, you can be almost certain that nearly everything is possible."

For best adaptability, Priebe recommends that theatres contract with lighting designers who can anticipate equipment for basic genres presented at that venue. Then, if management decides to change the genre in the future, they'll have a solid foundation to which they can make additions or modifications. To save money, Smith recommends purchasing used equipment, provided that parts and service are still available and the manufacturer has a good reputation.

If you choose a lighting vendor from outside your city, ask if they'll visit to consult with you. "We are more than happy to travel wherever is necessary to support our projects," says John Penisten, project manager for systems sales at Full Compass Systems, Ltd. The company provides audio, video and lighting sales and rentals from its home base in Middleton, Wis. Penisten notes, however, that vendors can often coordinate with architects, contractors and end users on small- and medium-sized projects without incurring travel costs for the client.

Finally, Salzberg urges theatres to hire a lighting *designer* rather than a *designer/electrician*. "Your theatre wasn't built by an architect/carpenter,'" he says, so pursuing someone specifically trained for the job is critical.

Making the best use of dimming products available, and what to add

Moving to the next step, how can you make the best of what you have while adding equipment that fits your budget? Smith recommends a forward-thinking attitude: "Solve real problems that have arisen in productions," he says. "Don't buy the latest and greatest being pushed by a consultant, dealer or product rep. Ask your lighting designers what they need."

This isn't meant as an insult to the vendors; rather, it's a practical approach: "Because most vendors are not trained designers," says Salzberg, "they're less likely to approach the task from a problem-solving point of view." In addition, Smith recommends querying your technicians, then adding their notes into the overall discussion about what to do.

As an example, Salzberg offers ideas on low-cost dimming equipment: "Shoebox dimmers can be purchased for less than $25 per dimmer," he says. "They can be plugged into available outlets." Search for used fixtures online at sites like eBay. As for controlling your dimmers, "there are several software/hardware packages that allow theatres to control stage lighting from a personal computer," says Salzberg. "Some of these are as flexible as more expensive dedicated consoles."

Theatres utilizing low-end systems are usually interested in products that are flexible, portable and work across many applications, says White. "As you move up into larger and more permanent applications—colleges, community theaters, local performing art centers—you move into higher fixture quantities, and therefore higher dimmer numbers."

And keep up with the latest technology as best you can. "Today facilities of all sizes are integrating automated lighting (either through purchase or rental), multimedia controls, and advanced Ethernet-based control protocols," says Rogers. "Many leading manufacturers are preparing to adopt Ethernet-based control protocols for the systems that will allow users to connect devices faster and easier than before."

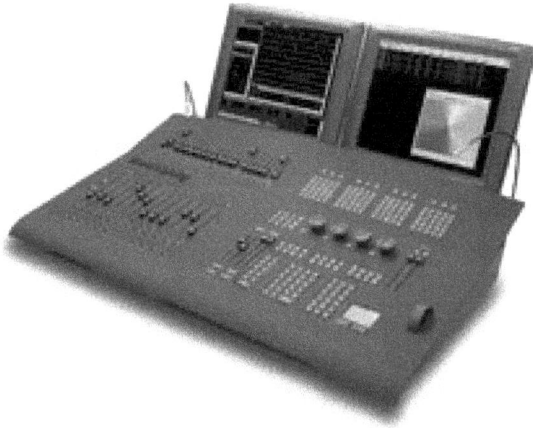

Lighting console from Strand. The VL is Strand's advanced moving light console. The direct action keypad speeds production with direct selection of lights, positions, colors or any other attribute. *(Photo courtesy of Strand Lighting)*

Will wireless work for you?

Certain types of venues can benefit greatly from wireless dimming. "It's particularly handy for repertory houses where multiple shows run concurrently," says Smith. Because many productions require items like table lamps, sconces, gas lanterns, special effect lighting, ringing telephones and puffs of smoke, a battery-powered wireless DMX dimmer inside each piece makes lighting simple and convenient.

Theme parks and specialty shows make use of wireless technology as well. "Shows that might be held on a barge or other remote area," says Priebe, "might choose wireless just to avoid having to operate the console at the spot of the performance." Wireless is a good choice when running DMX cable just isn't possible or when the cable might be an eyesore. Eliminating a control cable will also minimize the possibility of malfunctions and short-circuiting.

DMX-controlled dimmers are small and affordable, says Smith, who adds that it's relatively easy to install a 50-watt MR16 lamp "just about anywhere"—even inside a costume. "Wireless low-voltage dimmers are, for the first time ever, small enough to hide anywhere," adds Smith. "Now they're the size of a matchbox. Finally, a wireless DMX-controlled dimmer that fits in a candlestick!"

However, vendors and lighting designers caution that theatre administrators should look at wireless capability only as a final option. "Wireless is more expensive and less reliable than wired lighting," says Salzberg. Adds Priebe: "If your system is working just fine and there are no cable-related issues, it would not be cost-effective to make the change simply to 'go wireless.' However, convenience plays a factor in the ultimate decision at hand." Going wireless allows more versatility as far as control goes, he says.

No matter what the budget, Smith says that every theatre can benefit from purchasing a few low-voltage wireless dimmers. First, though, he urges administrators to ask the following questions: "Do you need a DMX feed in a location where there is no existing wiring? Do you need to put the main console in different positions for various utilizations of your space? Will you be touring your production into venues with questionable house DMX wiring?"

From a basic console with a traditional rack to a souped-up controller wired to an Ethernet network, dimming technology can suit any theatre's needs. Just remember a few key items when choosing or upgrading your equipment: "Purchase items that will directly, visibly, improve the viewer experience as a show unfolds on your stage," says James David Smith. "Do it with equipment that is reliable, serviceable, and affordable for you and your people."

Great Audio for your Theatre: Foolproof ways to guarantee the best in sound

Dispersion control. Acoustic interface. Audio fidelity. To technical personnel—sound designers and engineers—these words are music to the ears. But to theatre administrators, such phrases can be a cacophony of confusion. How can theatres ensure that their audiences are getting premium sound during show performances?

At a minimum, theatre managers need to be aware of "the acoustic qualities of their theatres, the capabilities of their sound systems, and what those factors taken together make their venue appropriate for," says sound engineer John Sibley, who is currently working on the new musical version of Mel Brooks' "Young Frankenstein."

Getting the proper guidance

To ensure that they have the proper audio ammunition, Jonathan Darling, senior consultant with Kirkegaard Associates in Chicago, Ill., recommends that theatres survey the types of productions that will be performed in the venue. Rely on a sound designer or consultant to provide guidance on equipment requirements for each type of performance.

"The sound designer can ensure that every word is heard, that nothing—no nuance, no subtle inflection, no muttered syllable—is lost," says Kai Harada, a New York-based sound designer who currently works as the sound supervisor for all productions of "Wicked" worldwide. Each production uses between 100 and 200 strategically placed loudspeakers.

For theatre managers who need help picking the best equipment for their facility, audio consultants stand ready to help. These consultants are "manufacturer-neutral," says Joe Ciaudelli, director of marketing at Sennheiser USA in Old Lyme, Conn. Consultants are entrusted with providing an objective analysis of what can fit within the client's budget. Edward Logsdon, a consultant with D.L. Adams Associates, Inc., in Denver, Colo., agrees: "It's hard to remain unbiased when you make money selling specific product lines," he says. After all, "we are the owner's advocate and trainer. We help them sleep well at night."

Identifying sound system weaknesses or poor acoustics

What factors can damage the acoustics in a theatre? "Cheap flooring, walls and carpet," says Harada, who works primarily in large-scale musicals that require gigantic sound systems. "The more reflective the walls, floors, and ceilings are," he says, "the more difficult it is to properly balance a sound system to work in that room."

Darling agrees, adding that house sound engineers need to have a solid understanding of loudspeaker design and how the loudspeakers interface with the acoustics of a venue. Improper equipment selection or placement can result in annoying

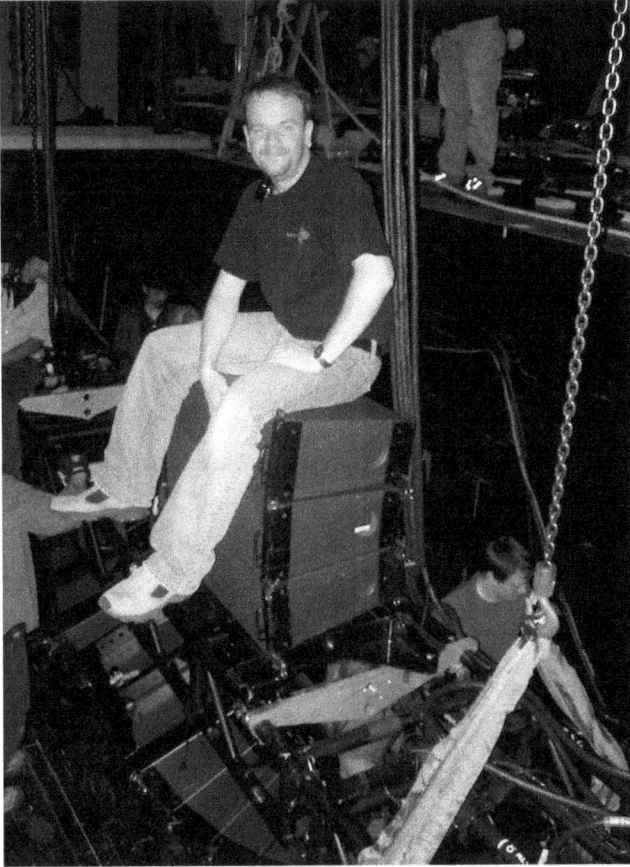

Installing a sound system for a touring show: Sound engineer
John Sibley. *(Photo courtesy of John Sibley)*

electronic feedback through the sound system in addition to
problems understanding the audio being transmitted through the
speakers.

As an audio consultant, Logsdon commonly deals with issues related to lack of sound coverage or operator error in working
the equipment. To avoid these problems, Logsdon uses computer
software like EASE, developed by the German firm Acoustic Design Ahnert, that simulates room acoustics using a 3-D model of
the room to help him map the placement of loudspeakers. As part

of his service to clients, Logsdon also provides extensive training on the equipment he designs for them.

According to Harada, another culprit of weak theatre acoustics is ambient noise—HVAC, lighting equipment, dimmer racks, the box office, the adjacent street, the parking lot outside. "As these sounds get louder, it becomes more and more challenging to ensure that the things the audience wants to hear are, in fact, being heard over the din."

How can theatres attack their existing sound issues? "Acousticians and engineers can work together to combat the problem," says Harada. The issues can include fixing noisy ductwork, double-insulating auditorium doors and remotely positioning air conditioning equipment. Harada also recommends that administrators invest some time and money to place lighting dimmers and stage automation equipment in separate, acoustically isolated locations in their theatres.

Making the most of what you have: basic considerations and simple upgrades

Combining the needs of the show with the right equipment can be a challenging experience. Does the show need spot sound effects or an all-encompassing soundscape? If the venue has a thrust stage, where should the loudspeakers be placed? Is there an orchestra pit, a balcony, boxes or a loge? Will music be performed on acoustic or electronic instruments? Harada deals with questions like these, and many more, in his daily work as a sound designer.

Sound engineer Sibley reveals the basic equipment requirements for any venue: "speaker coverage to every seat; sufficient console inputs for their style of production; paging, intercom and video for crew communication; basic SFX, playback, and recording abilities; and a console suitable for their needs and appropriate to the skill levels of their operators."

Would you like stereo playback? Surround sound? Or just even coverage across all of your seating? You might be surprised at how far your audio dollar can stretch. For example, says Ciaudelli, affixing sound-dampening material on large reflective surfaces like brick walls is a quick and inexpensive way of boosting the acoustical quality of your theatre. Kai Harada recalls a recent show in which a column in the balcony created nasty sound reflections for the several rows of seats in front of it. "After consulting with the theatre owners," he says, "we installed a small panel of carpeted material on the column which significantly cut down on the reflections."

If you need to replace battered old loudspeakers, "the modern generation of powered speakers comes with amplifiers built into the speaker cabinets"—providing terrific cost savings by deleting the need for separate amps, says Sibley. In addition, computer-controlled gear can simplify things as well: "A $600 PC can now take the place of racks and racks of expensive sound effects playback and recording hardware," he adds.

In the same vein, Logsdon advises that theatre managers start the upgrade process by examining their current loudspeaker set-up and its amplification quality. "Many times theatres don't have enough loudspeakers to properly cover the seating areas," he explains. If additional microphone inputs are needed, an economical solution is to add wireless microphones or an intercom system because wiring isn't required for anything except the antenna. Wireless technology can also be used to expand the theatre's intercom system.

New trends

What new audio technologies are on the horizon? "Digital, digital, digital," says Sibley. "Digital live consoles are taking the place of their analog brethren, ushering in a new era of compactness and unprecedented capabilities and flexibility." Speaker systems are networked together and computer-controlled, making life easier for the operator.

Things are changing in the academic arena as well. "I'm seeing many high school auditoriums using video projection with DVD and computer inputs for presentation use," says Logsdon. In addition, he says, many theatres are installing several different types of sound systems such as performance sound, surround sound and reverberation enhancement for maximum flexibility.

Sibley urges that no matter what you install, think about future expandability. "Wire is cheap compared to the cost of labor to run it; put in as much as you can afford," he says. Since the industry is moving to inexpensive CAT5 wiring standards for digital data, "run as much as you can to every location you can think of in a logical, easily patched manner. It will give you the infrastructure to expand easily as you grow."

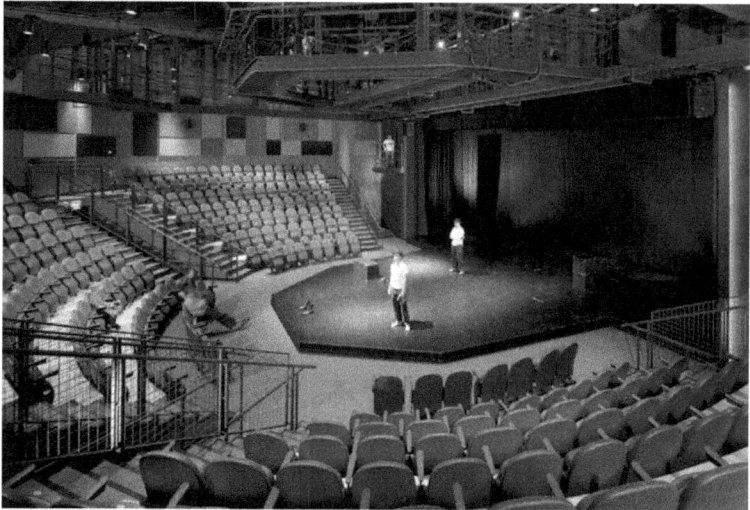

D.L. Adams Associates, a consulting firm based in Denver, Colorado, designed the acoustics for the 317-seat University Theatre at Colorado State University. Seating is arranged in three-quarter round. Consultant Ed Logsdon worked on the project. *(Photo courtesy of D.L. Adams Associates)*

Expert advice: how to make sure patrons hear perfectly

According to Darling, the Americans with Disabilities Act requires facilities with more than about 50 fixed seats to include hearing assistance systems for their patrons. "The system to choose depends on budget and some consideration of the audience percentage that will use the devices," he says.

Ciaudelli recommends the use of an infrared assistive listening system (ALS), which distributes sound throughout the venue via headsets, earphones or other devices. Sound designer Harada agrees; in fact, most of the theatres where he's worked feature this type of equipment. "The system is fed a mix of a mixing console output of the show along with a microphone located somewhere in the audience," he says.

According to Sibley, outfitting hard-of-hearing patrons with personal headsets is a cost-effective, durable and reliable way to ensure that the sounds of the show reach everyone in the audience. For theatres on a tighter budget, Sibley says, " there are FM-based headset systems such as those made by Williams, Comtek and Phonic Ear." Feeding these systems can be as simple as hanging a microphone above the stage of a small venue. Larger venues can place microphones around the stage and then mix the audio through a sound console.

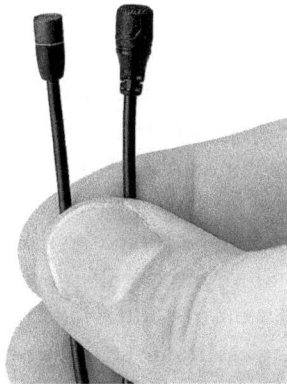

Sennheiser Gold Lavalier RF wireless microphone suitable for both speech and instrument miking applications in all areas of live work. A special Umbrella Diaphragm and a welded housing protect the microphone against sweat and moisture, making it useful for theatrical productions.
(Photo courtesy of Sennheiser USA)

Costs

Renovating or installing a new sound system in your theatre can vary widely in cost. Ciaudelli notes that the equipment falls into four main categories: acoustic treatment (sound-absorbing materials like diffusers and absorbers), microphones, control consoles and speakers. According to Darling, a black box theatre might spend $50,000 on a complete system renovation, while a 2,000-seat venue can spend $1 million or more.

Darling cautions that theatre administrators not confuse professional equipment for their theatre with home consumer gear, as they are two different animals. "It is common for people to equate costs between consumer and professional equipment and be very surprised by the size, cost and installation expense of professional systems," he says. The durability and much higher output requirements of professional equipment make it much more expensive. Also, he says, "the quality of the audio infrastructure including the power supply, cabling and termination is not well understood by many. Poor installation results in good equipment sounding bad because the infrastructure is of low quality."

Improving your theatre's sound isn't as difficult as it might seem. Consider the basics first; then look at costlier upgrades that can be phased in over time. This requires a master plan so the equipment and system are compatible with future additions. Logsdon notes that at a minimum theatres need to provide "good speech intelligibility, so the actors or presenters' voices can be easily heard and understood." And for best results, says Ciaudelli, start by improving the physical acoustics of the facility before trying to compensate by purchasing electronic equipment.

Theatre Flooring: Choosing and Maintaining the Perfect Surface

Whether your performers stroll, step, stand or dance on your venue's stage, selecting the right type of floor can make all the difference in performance quality and, consequently, ticket sales. At the Marjorie Luke Theatre in Santa Barbara, Calif., a recent $3 million renovation of the entire facility included a remodeling and extension of the stage. "We built out an area from the proscenium arch where we could store our steel deck under the front lip of the stage," explains Mark Robley Johnson, the theatre's technical director.

In a unique agreement, the theatre—located on the grounds of Santa Barbara Junior High School—is operated by a nonprofit organization as a dual-use facility. When not being used by the school, the facility hosts a wide variety of entertainment including children's theatre, acting workshops, dance presentations and musical acts.

Obtaining proper funding and finding time in a busy schedule can be huge roadblocks in the effort to overhaul your stage
floor. For some theatres this means raising money through various
means and then going dark for a while as the work gets underway.
The 10-month renovation of the Marjorie Luke Theatre—which
was originally built during the Great Depression—was a grass-
roots effort that blended private and corporate donations with
funding from a state initiative.

Like the theatre itself, the new stage floor is multipurpose. "It's
wood over concrete," explains Johnson. "Then we laid a masonite
cover on it. When we have dance presentations or groups that
request it, we lay down a Harlequin sprung floor." A "sprung" or
"floating" floor is engineered to provide appropriate cushion or
"bounce" for certain types of performances. Moorestown, N.J.-
based American Harlequin produces portable sprung floor panels
that can be stored when not in use.

On the other hand, perhaps your theatre needs a floor that
stays put, or maybe you're looking for an easy-to-clean surface to
cover an existing concrete subfloor. Whatever the case, flooring
vendors offer a wide variety of surface types, from black linoleum
to hardwood hewn from solid oak. Randy Swartz, president of
Philadelphia's Stagestep, Inc., provides a few examples: "Our Rave
flooring comes in lots of colors and is very lightweight," he says.
"Timestep, a heavy-duty flooring, is used for tap, hip-hop and theatrical productions where sets and props are used onstage. Quiet-
step is used primarily for ballet."

Is it time to replace your floor? If it's old and brittle, damaged
or stained beyond repair, or no longer lies flat, it's probably time
to call a flooring contractor. According to Tracey Cosgrove, product manager for Rosco Laboratories in Stamford, Conn., theatres
need to focus on several key questions when hunting for a company to install a new stage floor: "First, what kinds of activities
are going to happen on the floor? Will there be dancing, classes,
or scenery moved across it? And second, is the floor a permanent
install, or will it be a temporary floor that will be moved on and
off the stage, or in and out of a facility?" Adds Claire Londress of

Stagestep's Super Bravo flooring in a studio at New York University's Tisch School of the Arts. *(Photo courtesy of Stagestep)*

American Harlequin, "We need to know about the current subfloor in the facility. Is it a hard subfloor like concrete, wood or tile? Or is it a sprung floor instead?"

Your most useful tool in choosing a new floor is to talk to those who will use it the most. Of course, opinions will vary depending on whom you're asking. "Lighting designers like non-reflective floors and generally like black," says Randy Swartz of Stagestep. "On the other hand, dancers usually prefer gray flooring, which gives them a horizon." Renae Williams, the director of dance presentation at the Los Angeles Music Center, took a democratic approach to choosing a new stage floor for her facility: "Our Technical Director researched several different options and also spoke with the production staff from the companies we present. We want our visiting artists to feel comfortable and well taken care of while here."

At the Chautauqua Institution, an educational facility and resort in New York, the newly christened Bratton Theatre sports a brand-new stage. "The old theatre was a very small converted space," says Mike Sullivan, director of institution relations. "It didn't have a real stage, and it had temporary seating. Our theatre company was very good at putting on these wonderful plays and really needed a space to match their talent." Funded through a capital campaign, consultants Davis Crossfield Associates and architect Mitchell Kurtz reworked the space into a true theatre.

According to Kurtz, the Bratton Theatre's new stage was crafted with ordinary carpentry materials. "Whatever you might carve up, you can simply get a replacement piece from a lumber yard," he says. The top quarter-inch of the floor is "sacrificial" or replaceable. "So as you screw into the floor over the years," explains Kurtz, "you can peel the layers apart and toss them away without undermining the structure." Adds Robert Davis of Davis Crossfield Associates, "If you paint on the surface with a thick paint that won't come off, you don't have to spend hours scraping it. You just have to replace the panels."

When talking with a flooring contractor, make sure you've decided how much surface coverage you require. "We've done stages as small as 750 square feet for high school theatres," says Graves, "and as large as 20,000 square feet for concert halls." Larger venues require additional flooring because of their multipurpose requirements, wings, and the like. Keep an eye on cost as you add up your space requirements. According to Swartz, floors by Stagestep can run between $1.22 to $3.89 per square foot, with additional costs for shipping, subfloors, and adhesives.

Protecting your investment

While the major manufacturers all provide some type of warranty for new floors, a theatre's first line of defense is to maintain the surface with care. "If it isn't maintained properly," cautions Graves, "a new floor can be destroyed fairly quickly"—sometimes in as little as three years. Entertainment Flooring Systems provides a one-year warranty for hardwood floors due to their propensity for easy wear and tear. Vinyl and linoleum, on the other hand, come with a seven-year warranty. At Rosco Laboratories, the typical warranty is five years against manufacturing defects, while American Harlequin offers a lifetime warranty.

The materials used in the construction of the floor play a large role in its lifespan. Graves notes that while hardwood can last for many years, vinyl and linoleum floors exist in a constant state of wear-and-tear and will eventually dry out. "Vinyl hardens and becomes brittle," says Graves, "because the plasticizers, which keep the surface flexible, are constantly curing. Linoleum eventually dries out too." He estimates that well-maintained vinyl can last eight to 15 years under normal wear conditions. Adds Davis, "There are many serviceable floors that are 50 years old or older. It depends on how you use them."

Is your theatre part of the green building movement? If you prefer to use as many ecology-friendly products as possible, you have some additional items to consider when choosing your new stage floor. Linoleum (a canvas or burlap base covered with linseed oil and other materials) and vinyl (a synthetic plastic composed of chlorine and ethylene derivatives) are less expensive than natural wood. Critical to choosing a "green" floor are the materials used in manufacturing and installation, as well as factors like toxicity, recyclability and longevity.

Speaking of recycling, the Cleveland Public Theatre took an interesting approach when it resurfaced the stage of its Gordon Square Theatre several years ago. "We are slowly renovating the properties," says Executive Artistic Director Raymond Bobgan, "and are now undertaking a major capital campaign in cooperation with a community development organization and another theatre." Volunteers and several designers visited a nearby racquetball court that was being torn down. "We took the racquetball floor apart so it wouldn't be destroyed," recalls Bobgan, "and then installed it over the floor of the Gordon Square Theatre."

To keep your new floor sparkling, soap- and wax-based cleaners are not recommended for surfaces like vinyl because the cleaner will make the floor slippery—which spells certain disaster for the performer. "For vinyl surfaces, we recommend the use of a pH-neutral vinyl floor cleaner," says Claire Londress of Harlequin. "This type of cleaner can be found at almost any hardware or home supply store." Londress cautions that while buffing machines are useful for large areas, the equipment must be used carefully to avoid damaging the non-slip surface. According to Graves, hardwood floors, despite their longevity, can require refinishing up to twice a year—an additional cost for the theatre.

Installing a new floor

At Entertainment Flooring Systems, Michael Sean Graves supervises the installation of each floor, usually with a team of stagehands with whom he's worked for the last two decades. "Sometimes we use local labor as well," he says. "It depends on where the space is and the availability of my experienced labor." On average the team can install approximately 1000 square feet of flooring per day. However, if two layers are required—for example, a sprung subfloor topped with a vinyl surface—the installers need twice the time to cover the same amount of surface area. For hardwood floors, Graves says that coverage decreases to 750 square feet per day because the crew needs to apply a coat of polyurethane to seal the new surface.

Once the stage is installed, it needs curing, or drying, time. According to Graves, glue used in linoleum or vinyl flooring typically takes at least a day to cure: "You need to wait 24 hours before you walk on it, and 48 hours until there's any major traffic on the surface." Heavy or rolling loads must wait one week before traversing the new stage.

For smooth installation of a new floor, Graves makes sure to chat with the client as well as the architect. "A lot of the time we deal with the architect or consultant, but we also need to consult with the owner of the facility. Sometimes with renovations, they way things are designed and the way they're used are totally different." Says Claire Londress, "We work with our customers to ensure that the design of the new floor suits existing space or, if we're looking at a new building, meshes with the architect's plans." For a great performance, the right environment can make all the difference.

12 Questions to Ask Before You Buy Your Next Theatre Floor

1. What types of performances will my theatre be presenting?
2. Does the floor need to be portable, or is a permanent installation sufficient for my needs?
3. What is my available budget?
4. What type of subfloor do I currently have on my stage or performance area?
5. What type of surface do I prefer — hardwood or a plastic like vinyl — and is it the best type for the performers who will use it?
6. How does the floor look from a distance, and what will the audience see?
7. How much surface area will the floor need to cover?
8. How long do I need this new floor to last?
9. What particular requirements do I have—a certain color, sound and light absorption, type of insulation, environmentally friendly construction materials?
10. How can I maintain and clean this new floor?
11. What type of warranty does the manufacturer offer?
12. Does my schedule mesh with the time requirements for installation and curing before I can use the floor?

Staging the Perfect Performance:
Using lifts, risers and fillers to raise the bar on your production

Expanding the surface area of your stage? Looking for a clever way for actors and props to appear and then disappear during a show? From hand-installed platforms to mechanically operated lifts, a variety of staging products provide clever ways to maximize theatre space and add production value to even the most basic theatrical presentation.

A variety of choices are available depending on your theatre's requirements and available budget. Vendors like StageRight Corporation in Clare, Mich., create portable staging equipment like choral, band and seating risers; pit fillers; orchestra enclosures; acoustical shells; and trap floor covers. According to Kathleen Meadowcroft, sales research specialist and trade show manager for the company, the firm benefits from having its manufacturing and distributing operations located under one roof. Similarly, Serapid, Inc., builds equipment like its LinkLift series of theatrical lifts at its facility in Sterling Heights, Mich., a suburb of Detroit.

Types of products for various configurations

No theatre wants to use cumbersome equipment, especially if the available space is limited. To that end, vendors including Minneapolis, Minn.-based Staging Concepts work to create products that are easy to use and make the most of a particular venue's physical infrastructure. "Our SC90 platforms are modular," says Kari Hayden, western sales manager for Staging Concepts. "The SC90 Legs can be made in adjustable heights or specific fixed heights, and our bridging understructures allow for quick setup and ample storage space beneath the stage."

Lifts are a basic mechanical system that can be adapted to a variety of uses, boosting production value and the venue's versatility as well. "A lift system helps make the theatre marketable to a variety of shows," says Ann Marie Fortunate, marketing manager for Serapid. "The lift can be used to extend the size of the stage or create additional seating depending on where the elevation of the lift is set." In addition, lifts can move production equipment on or off the stage or to and from storage areas. Most recently Serapid's lifts were installed in the Orange County Performing Arts Center in Costa Mesa, Calif., and at the Walt Disney Concert Hall in Los Angeles.

Mechanical lifts are useful for smooth scene changes. "The benefit for directors is the ability to change locations and prop elements quickly," says David Cap, production manager at the Arizona Theatre Company in Tucson, Ariz. "Often the lifts can be used for entrances by actors, making transitions smoother and quicker." Cap has used elevators for productions of "Jekyll and Hyde" and "Sherlock Holmes" to bring furniture elements up to the stage. For "Much Ado About Nothing," the Arizona Theatre Company used two lifts: one for actors and furniture, and the other for a fountain.

During the Broadway musical production of "Titanic," Gala Systems' Spiralifts helped simulate the sinking of the gigantic ocean liner onstage. According to Christopher Shaw, sales manager for Gala Systems in St-Hubert, Quebec, Canada, the introduction of the Spiralift in the late 1980s was revolutionary in the industry. "It was originally designed for theatrical use, specifically for orchestra lifts," he notes, "and has since been used in industrial applications."

Until the introduction of the Spiralift, Shaw continues, most theatre lifts used either hydraulic rams or bevel screw jacks—systems that required a deep pit and caissons (chambers) to enclose the ram or screw that drove the lift system. The Spiralift, by contrast, uses a more compact piece of technology: a coiled steel spring that expands as a low-power motor purrs away. This tool allows theatres to, for example, raise an orchestra 10 feet from a pit that is only two feet deep.

A production of "Sherlock Holmes" by the Arizona Theatre Company. According to Production Manager David Cap, elevators were used to bring furniture elements up to the stage.
(Photo courtesy of the Arizona Theatre Company)

For venues with smaller budgets that preclude such automation, Dan Culhane, engineering manager at SECOA, Inc., in Champlin, Minn., recommends the orchestra pit filler as a simple, cost-effective way to modify the physical infrastructure. "The stage floor is one of the most important scenic elements for any designer to use," says Culhane. "Having an orchestra pit filler increases the floor area significantly."

In addition, pit fillers provide greater flexibility, allowing scenic elements and actors to appear from underneath the stage. "Many orchestra pit fillers can be designed so that there is a maximum of open floor space below," says Culhane. "This allows for an orchestra to be in the pit area and still have an extended stage floor area above."

Culhane notes that orchestra pit fillers are probably the lowest cost for the return on investment in the high school and college market. The pit fillers "provide and deliver the ability to project the actor or speaker forward toward the audience allowing for a more intimate audience experience," he explains.

Culhane also recommends the use of stage traps. SECOA installed its largest trap system at the Guthrie Theatre in Minneapolis. "It's actually two systems: one for the proscenium stage and a second for the thrust stage," he explains. The proscenium's 48'-by-24' system consists of 72 individual 4'-by-4' modules, while the 880-square-foot thrust uses 54 modules. The entire aluminum system is removable and can withstand a fully loaded 14,000-pound forklift driving over its surface.

Go it alone, or work with consultants?

While smaller, simpler pieces of equipment can be set up and operated without much fuss, the installation of larger and more technical staging gear can benefit by hiring a consultant or technician to advise and oversee the process.

Previously the Arizona Theatre Company experimented with using consultants and with "going it alone." Currently the organization contracts with a local automation expert to help with its productions. As for whether to buy or rent the equipment, budget and space restrictions play a key role, as always. "Currently we rent motors and lifts from a local company," says Cap. "They have

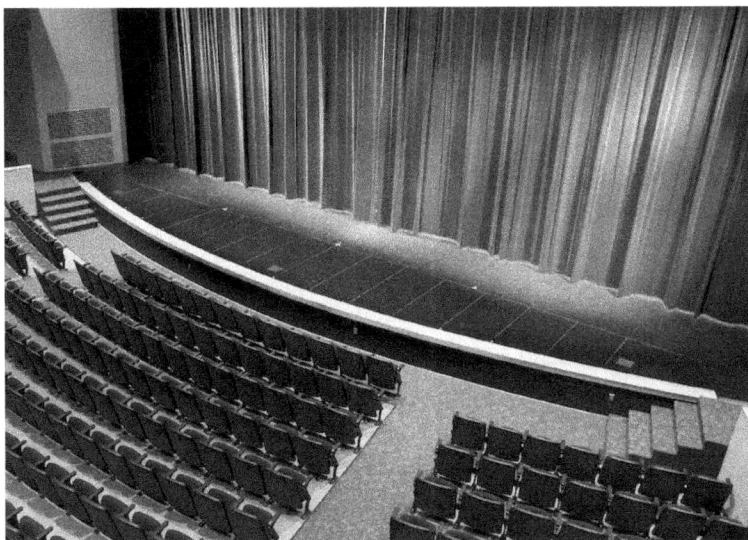

SECOA pit filler from Hopkins High School in Hopkins, Minnesota. *(Photo courtesy of SECOA, Inc.)*

worked with us for many years and have pieces tailored to our spaces."

Vendors also bring in the big guns to advise and design the staging products that they create for theatres around the world. Serapid works with consultants, architects and engineers—among other experts—throughout the design process to ensure that the staging equipment is the best choice for a particular venue. Meanwhile, Staging Concepts employs eight degreed engineers on staff and consults with other engineers as needed.

Construction materials and acoustics also play a large role in selecting a certain type of staging product. For example, says Culhane, SECOA offers pit fillers and stage traps featuring either an aluminum frame topped with a replaceable wood deck or a laminated stress-skin construction. If the walking surface gets damaged, the wood deck of the aluminum frame can be replaced. However, if the walking surface of the more expensive laminated deck is damaged, the theatre would need to swap out the entire deck.

On the other hand, an aluminum frame/wood deck with sound insulation is better at muffling the sounds of actors' footsteps as they move across the stage. Which one is right for your theatre and budget? A consultant can help you make the right choice.

Good advice about use, training and operation

Given all of these options, where should theatre administrators start when considering the purchase or rental of new staging equipment? Depending on the theatre's needs, sales managers and consultants can roll through a variety of product offerings that fit the bill. "For example, if our customers need an extremely quick set up and strike for their stage," says Hayden, "we recommend using bridge supports for understructures. If they need a stage that can be set up by only one person, we recommend our SC9000 EZ Stage. If there is a black box theatre that needs flexible seating, we would recommend the SC2000 seating riser system."

Theatres should also remember that their physical infrastructure might need some modification as well. If a theatre is considering adding a lift like ours and it is an existing space," says Shaw, "they need to realize that they may have some excavation to perform, electrical wiring requirements and other infrastructure needs. We are more than happy to answer any of their questions and offer suggestions."

Staging equipment can provide distinct advantages for a theatre's audience as well as its box office. "Stage managers and theatre directors should think about the type of productions the theatre currently hosts," says Fortunate. "If the space can be re-configured with a lift system, it can accommodate many different types of productions." In addition, she says, lift systems will also help increase sightlines for audience members. With some careful layout design, theatres can "facilitate the best view for everyone in the house."

Electrical and safety issues must be solved before new equipment is installed. Do not do cheap," urges Cap. "Pay attention to emergency stops." To avoid potential accidents, he recommends that elevator controls be tied into emergency stops built into the system. Also, "whether you are using AC or DC power affects emergency stops and procedures for power loss," Cap explains.

And of course, says Hayden, please read the instructions. "While our equipment is modular and very easy to use, we do recommend reading the set up instructions, as these will often answer any questions one may have."

Once you've installed your staging systems, strong communication will ensure a production that makes the most of the new lifts, platforms and other assorted gear. "Be clear and concise with stage management, directors and actors about the procedures and actions of the moving pieces," says Cap. Whether you're simply erecting a group of modular platforms to extend your stage, or bolting in a lift system to make the orchestra rise upward, choosing the right staging equipment will increase the flexibility and creativity of your productions while boosting your theatre's public profile in the marketplace.

Staging Concepts' SC2000 seating riser system.
(Photo courtesy of Serapid, Inc.)

The Detail is in the Props:
Make your production pop
with the right props

Preparing for a production? Make sure that you're acquiring the right props. Swords-and-firearms expert Richard Pallaziol, president of Weapons of Choice, a Napa, Calif.-based prop supplier, knows what can happen when the prop list is vague or hasn't been carefully researched. Recently a props person came to Pallaziol with a request for a 35-millimeter revolver—an item that doesn't exist except as an antiaircraft gun. "When shown a photo of one, mounted on a destroyer and standing 15 feet tall, the designer relented," chuckles Pallaziol.

The importance of props

Having the right props in the right places can make all the difference in your audience's ability to suspend disbelief. "Choosing a prop can't be left to chance," says John C. McIlwee, director of theatre at North Carolina State University in Raleigh, N.C. "Once cannot choose any old lamp or table that may take the audience eye out of the Ã"world' the designer created."

Kristen Morgan-Johnson, instructor of scenic technology in the theatre arts department at Virginia Tech University, agrees: "A good prop can make or break a pivotal scene in a performance. Imagine a fight scene from any Shakespeare with the wrong weapon, or an obvious out-of-period piece that doesn't match." Errors like these yank the audience out of the action and make them focus on the prop—or, in some cases, the lack of one.

Bringing the prop to life

So how can the set designer and director ensure that they create a believable "world" onstage? "I usually run each prop by both of them," says Adriane Roberts, properties master at Theatreworks, a repertory theatre in Palo Alto, Calif. The designer tells Roberts what the prop looks like, while the director tells her how the prop will be used. Before a show opens Roberts sits down with the assistant stage manager and prop crew head to review every prop and its function.

To ensure accuracy, Pallaziol recommends doing thorough research backed by lots of pictures. It also helps to tell each prop's "story," says Bill Turner, general manager of The National Theatre for Children in Minneapolis, Minn. "Communicate what the prop is supposed to do.' Why is it there, what does it mean to the characters, what should it mean to the audience?" While intricate detail isn't usually necessary, "if a key detail is missing, the production—and some poor member of the production staff—suffers," he adds. "It helps designers to have a 'why.'"

Even after being as thorough as possible, says Pallaziol, be prepared to have designers or directors change their minds when they see the actual prop. "Theatre is visual, and no amount of description can substitute for showing and using the item in front of them," he says. At the Steppenwolf Theatre Company in Chicago, Ill., "We give the actors as many of the real' or show props that we have so they can get used to them in rehearsal," says Prop Master Jenny DiLuciano. If the actual prop is unavailable, DiLuciano provides something to approximate it while she shops for or builds the real thing.

Coburn Goss (left) and Polly Noonan (right) in "Dead Man's Cell Phone" by Sarah Ruhl, directed by Jessica Thebus at Steppenwolf Theatre, March 27-July 27, 2008.
(Photo courtesy of Steppenwolf Theatre Company)

Rent or buy?

If you don't already have the prop in your own collection, should you rent or buy what you need? "Rent!" urges Turner. "Are you really going to use that lute in another show?" he says, recalling a decision he made in 1998 that haunts him to this day. Roberts notes that renting is cheaper in the long run. However, she adds, "You are usually more limited in what you can do to the prop. Nice chair, but I can't reupholster or paint it." By contrast, purchasing a prop costs more but you can modify it as you see fit.

Pallaziol says that depending on the typical season of shows, theatres might be wise to own rather than rent certain props. For example, he says, "If you do a lot of Shakespeare, you should probably keep some generic swords. But at the end of each production, take a good hard look at each prop that you now own and decide if there is a strong chance that the item will be used again in the next five years. If the answer is 'no,' or even 'maybe,' get rid of it." With ever increasing warehouse costs, notes Pallaziol, storing a prop can prove far more costly than simply renting one.

Find or build?

Searching for the right props can be an adventure. "First," says Pallaziol, "get on the phone and start bothering all of the other theatres in the area." If they have what you need, he says, you've just saved a lot of time and money. "Network with historical societies and other theatres," adds Turner. "You never know who's going to have that perfect period item." If it's appropriate to your theatre, you can even ask for help from donors and audience members.

Secondhand stores and antique shops might carry what you need for your production—or at the very least an item that can be modified for your use. "I shop online, in retail stores, flea markets, thrift stores and even garage sales," says Andrew Lewis, owner of The Prop House in San Francisco, Calif. "Sometimes I fabricate from scratch or modify existing props."

At Virginia Tech, Morgan-Johnson pulls what she can from existing stock, then buys or builds the remaining props. A production of "Graceland" called for an Elvis-shaped liquor bottle and a pillow featuring Elvis' face stitched in needlepoint. After scouring local antique stores and coming up empty-handed, Morgan-Johnson did some Internet shopping and found the items on eBay.

Management and storage

While a computerized database is the most obvious inventory tool, often a prop collection changes too fast for the staff to keep up. "A computer database is a pipe dream for most prop shops,"

In a 2007 production of "Joe Turner's Come and Gone," a great deal of the action was set in a working kitchen. "The set dressing really made the difference in turning a theatrical set into what the audience accepted as a period kitchen," says Kristen Morgan-Johnson, instructor of scenic technology in the theatre arts department at Virginia Tech University.
(Photo courtesy of Virginia Tech University)

says Roberts. "With eight shows a season we have a constantly changing inventory."

At The Prop House, Lewis manages his 20,000 square feet of items the old-fashioned way: "mostly in my head," he laughs, "but I do have a Web site with a partial online inventory." The National Theatre for Children runs a full computer inventory each year and stores its props in a series of boxes containing like items.

In Chicago the Steppenwolf Theatre Company has an area for furniture, a separate area for smaller items or hand props, and another area for fabric, bedding and pillows. "We have lots of shelving units full of large clear plastic bins (so you can see what's inside) with lids (to keep the dust out)," says DiLuciano. Like items are kept in each bin. There's also a furniture area where items like dining room tables, sofas and beds are grouped together. While not everything is listed in a computer database yet, DiLuciano notes that it would take an additional full-time staffer to photograph, catalog and inventory everything in the rapidly-changing collection. "As it is now we have to take advantage of pockets of time when we're not working on a show to maintain order in these areas," she says.

"The best inventory I've seen was a furniture-only inventory that was a picture database that designers could access on the Web," says Roberts. "Furniture doesn't change as much as small prop storage does." But until there's more time, money and staff, prop shops keep up with inventory as best they can. "We just try to keep things properly labeled and in a place where we can find them for the next show they're needed for," she adds.

Making money from your prop collection

If your prop collection is good-sized, or you have a small number of interesting pieces, you might consider running a rental program yourself. Making money from your props is all in the marketing, says Pallaziol: "Get your name out there," he says. "Work up a flyer with a list of what you have and mail it to local and regional theatres. If you have built good-looking and reliable blood razors for 'Sweeney Todd,' tell everybody."

Your rental inventory should be limited to items that will be used frequently, says Turner. He urges theatres to avoid acquiring specialty items specifically for a rental program unless they have plenty of storage space and can obtain the items cheaply.

At Weapons of Choice, Pallaziol views his job as monitoring a constant flow of shipments rather than simply maintaining a warehouse. "Items are spoken for at least three productions in advance," he says. "Most of our props are on a rack here for only a day or two, and we rarely have more than five percent of our inventory actually in our hands at any given moment." None of this would be possible without a computerized system.

Consider your pricing structure and potential customer base: "Who in my community is going to rent from me?" says Turner. "Professional theatres? Community theatres?" Pallaziol recommends that theatres estimate the replacement cost—the purchase price or material plus labor—and set a monthly rate somewhere between one-tenth to one-quarter of that value. "Don't be greedy," he says. "Remember that you want to recoup some of your cost, not make a killing. And better that you get $20 now than wait for $100 that no one will pay. After all, every day that your prop sits and takes up space is costing you money."

Finally, keep an eye out for props that you can add to your collection. You never know when they'll come in handy. "I have my own prop house, but I cannot possibly have every prop that could ever be needed," says Lewis. "So I am always shopping for just the right prop needed for that particular scene." Remember also that the actors need to feel comfortable interacting with the items that you provide. A little extra time and communication will ensure that the right prop is in the right place.

A Doll With Safety Issues
How a seemingly innocent prop can cause harm—and how to keep it from happening

"When getting or building a period prop," says Richard Pallaziol of Weapons of Choice, "remember that you may still need to modify it to serve your production. In 'The Miracle Worker,' for instance, Helen strikes Anne with a doll. The perfect doll for the period would be one with a ceramic head sewn onto a fabric body."

"Well, there is no way that a true doll like that can strike someone and not risk grievous injury. So you'll have to find a soft rubber head instead. Even then, think about how the prop is going to be used and rebuilt for all worst-case scenarios. The head on that same doll can easily rip from the fabric and fly out into the audience. (Trust me, it's happened.) So you'll need not only to sew the head onto the body with fishing line, but also run the fishing line all the way down to the doll's feet."

SFX—Size Doesn't Matter:
From flying to fog, make special effects work for you, whatever your stage size

At the Public Theater in New York City, the Labyrinth Theatre Company is staging a production of "Unconditional," an ensemble play about racial issues. The play is performed in the round with a maximum audience of 90. Onstage an angry man torments another by forcing the latter to stand on a chair with a hangman's noose around his neck. On the floor nearby, a Confederate flag burns brightly in a small trashcan.

This was no simulated effect: the fire was real—created by mounting a custom-designed flame tray and a small fog machine inside the trashcan. "The actor and I worked together over the tech process to ensure his understanding and control over how to safely light it and treat open flame on the stage," says Jeremy Chernick, design associate for J&M Special Effects in Brooklyn, N.Y.

Whether it's fire, fog, smoke or water, crafting eye-popping special effects is a challenge for any production, large or small.

And fitting SFX into tight or unconventional spaces takes an expert designer who knows where and how to install tools like fans, strobe lights and even snow machines. Effects can be motorized, pneumatically driven, and computer-controlled; but in the end, safety and reliability must blend with effective SFX to ensure that the audience believes in the illusion.

Burning a fire in a trashcan wasn't the only effect J&M created for "Unconditional." Chernick also had to simulate the hanging of a man onstage. "We used a specially built stunt harness and a noose with hidden support and safety cables hidden inside," he explains. "A special one-foot by ten-foot box truss was installed onto the grid, and we had a highly experienced and trained rigger install all aspects of the effect." Clever lighting to redirect the audience's eye completed the illusion.

Overcoming space limitations

According to SFX designers, careful planning from the outset is critical. "Often," says Chernick, "special effects are added into a show after all other areas have been designed. This makes for a lot of complicated and ingenious thinking as we often have to work around the set or lighting, instead of the other way around."

Sometimes the simple approach to SFX works best. In the spring of 2006, Peter Wood, a special effects designer from Monrovia, Md., designed the environment for the gothic puppet-driven drama "Victor Frankenstein," performed at the University of Maryland, Baltimore County. Effects included fire and chilled fog that raced across the stage. In building the set and effects for the show, Wood faced a daunting roadblock: the theatre ceiling was only 13 feet high and lacked a fly loft.

In certain scenes, curtains needed to appear in the background to suggest a window. "Since the theatre wasn't equipped with a loft, I suggested we use a motorized system that would roll the curtain up on cue, like an electric window shade," recalls Wood. After researching different motors and control units, "I joked that we should just hack apart one of our DeWalt cordless drills and use its motor and switch." This turned out to be the solution to the problem, as it provided a reliable motor and a variable-speed switch for controlling the curtain effect.

What if your actors need to float across the stage, as in productions of "Wicked" and "Peter Pan"? Well-established companies like ZFX Flying Effects in Louisville, Ky., and Flying By Foy in Las Vegas, Nev., can adapt their equipment to indoor and outdoor venues and ceilings high or low. "As long as there is a secure structure to which we can attach our systems," says Tracy Nunnally, president of Hall Associates in Dekalb, Ill., "you can fly."

In fact, special effects experts say they can make almost anything happen despite the size or shape of the stage. "The size of the space should not limit what can be done as long as everyone works together," says Chernick.

Special effects designer Peter Wood on the set of "Victor Frankenstein" at the University of Maryland, Baltimore County.
(Photo courtesy of Peter Wood Productions)

75

Finding an alternate solution

For small budgets in small theatres, workarounds are readily available. "There are easy and cheaper alternatives too many large effects that smaller production companies may not know about," says Chernick. "This may mean a healthy imagination, or a more theatrical choice as opposed to realism, but there are a lots of possibilities—just ask a professional."

Using water can be a challenging and sometimes messy endeavor. Doug Adams, president of Pyrotek Special Effects in Las Vegas, Nev., has created effects for large shows like "Phantom of the Opera," "Cats" and "The Rocky Horror Picture Show." Through another one of his companies, Aqua Visual FX, Adams provides theatres of all sizes with liquid effects via connectable modules that create various lengths of water screens. A surface can be added to project laser graphics and 3-D multimedia images.

"It's a standalone item—a 'water billboard' that drops pixilated water downward as the system creates shapes, lettering and logos on the water screen," explains Adams. If a theatre wants to avoid using real water in a production, Adams recommends using a black sharkstooth scrim and projecting images on it. "We also create effects on drop curtains," he adds.

While small performance spaces require creativity and improvisation on the part of the SFX designer, sometimes a stage can be too *large*. During a production that featured Dr. Seuss musical numbers, "I decided that many scenes would put a black art environment to good use," says Wood, "but our budget wasn't big enough to bath the entire stage in ultraviolet light." His solution was a black art "window," approximately eight feet square, which was cut into the set upstage center. Behind this archway was a black curtain; the entire frame was lined with fluorescent ultraviolet lights on the upstage side.

But even in this comparatively generous space Wood was faced with space restrictions: "When the script called for the Lorax to fly away, we built a large rolling rig and covered it in black cloth, which was invisible to the audience. In this case, the width of the stage was a limitation."

Challenges, creativity and improvisation

Programmed effects are even more important in performance spaces that are small or oddly shaped. Linda Batwin, co-creative director for Batwin + Robin Productions in New York, uses 3-D drawings of the theatre along with scenic drawings to get a sense of how the special effects are seen by the audience. By using these tools, "you also get a sense of scale of the screens and the movement," she explains. In addition, her team uses AfterEffects animation software to view how the stage movement, set, props and media work together.

"Doing a mock-up, either full scale or partial scale, is always the way to go," says Batwin. "It really helps you know what will work and what will not—and then you can go create it." The production of "Frank Sinatra: His Voice, His World, His Way" at Radio City Music Hall included a live 40-piece orchestra, imagery, film footage and an ensemble of singers and performers. During the planning stages, Batwin used AfterEffects to simulate what the show would look like. "It helps for the director, scenic designer and the media designers to be on the same page," says Batwin.

Fog machines, a part of the SFX toolbox for decades, can suddenly find themselves less effective than usual when challenged by newer technology. "Many newer buildings use a sophisticated smoke detection system that is particle-based, where sensors in the ductwork detect if many large particles appear in the air—presumably smoke," says Wood. This improvement in safety can wreak havoc on fog machines, especially in smaller venues where the SFX are closer to the smoke detection system.

As a workaround, Wood uses low-lying and quick-dissipating fog. "Chilled fog hugs the ground because it's cooler than the room temperature," he explains, "so by the time it's warmed up and is rising near the air intake, it has dissipated entirely." Wood also makes sure to use fog fluid that has been specially formulated to disperse quickly. "I like these solutions because the fog effect appears just as I had envisioned it," says Wood, "but also caters to the limitations of the venue's safety systems."

Safety issues in a small environment

Trained and licensed professionals in special effects are essential in creating suitable and safe moments for any sized venue, says Chernick. "Often the most spectacular moments occur in the smallest of spaces." Adams agrees: "You have to be aware of the trim height of the truss or fly galley, for example when you're dropping in scenic pieces," he cautions. "If you're using pyrotechnics, you have to make sure no sparks go past the dissipation point."

Adams points to a special effect his company installed on the stage of the Kodak Theatre in Los Angeles for the Academy Awards several years ago. With singers and dancers performing onstage, Adams and his team had to create artificial falling snow and trigger an automobile to explode during the performance. The car was just 15 feet from the audience—barely a comfortable minimum, says Adams. Moreover, lightning-fast scene changes increased the possibility of an accident. "Any materials you use have to be very quick to dissipate, with no fallout residue, and very easy to control," he says.

After rigorous testing in his Las Vegas headquarters, Adams moved the equipment to Los Angeles, where he reviewed it with the fire marshal. "We work very closely with the fire marshal," he says. "We go over everything with the artist and everyone else onstage before we do it. There's a lot of testing and calculations."

This attention to safety pays off in the long run. "Make sure you are being safe, legal, and never risking danger," says Chernick. "I suggest at least working with a professional as a consultant. Never use flame or pyrotechnics without a pyrotechnician or an explicit permit from your local fire department." In New York City, he says, open-flame permits are required for lighters, matches and cigarettes.

Squeezing special effects into any size venue is an art as well as a science. "Everything is possible," says Chernick, "but time and careful planning are important."

Costume Troubleshooting:
Stopping a train wreck before it happens

Onstage the cast of "Grease" sang and danced their way through another act. In one of the wings, Leslie Darling was frantically threading a needle with a long piece of sturdy thread. Standing in front of her was a cast member with an awkward costume malfunction: during his previous scene, which required him to walk with his pants around his ankles, he had ripped the zipper out of the front of his trousers.

"I worked summer stock for 20 years," says Darling. "The same guy would break his zipper every time. I'd be there to stitch him up until the end of the show." There was no time to whip off the pants and repair them with a sewing machine; Darling had to improvise. As she had many times before, she sewed up the actor and sent him on his way.

Last-minute costume emergencies like this are nothing new for Darling, the costume shop manager at Tracy Theatre Originals in Hampton, N.H., and for thousands of other designers who constantly tread the delicate line between creating breathtaking wardrobes for current shows and keeping them in good working order for future ones. After all, as some designers contend, the wardrobe can make or break a show.

As a supplier of every type of costume from opera dresses to the six-foot bunny at the annual White House Easter Egg Hunt, Jonn Schenz is a firm believer that properly measured, fitted and maintained wardrobe is the key to a successful production. Schenz founded his company, Schenz Theatrical Supply, Inc., 40 years ago in Cincinnati, Ohio.

Originally trained as a dancer, Schenz came to rely on his wardrobe to help him get in character no matter what show he was doing. "We worked in rep, and we did three different shows at the same time," he remembers. "Sometimes you have to stop and think, 'Who am I in this show'? When you put on that wardrobe, you know who you are."

For this reason, there's a lot riding on the costume designer's skill and quick thinking. "My job is make sure things get to theatre on time, and as close to budget as possible," says Callie Floor, manager of the costume rental program at the American Conservatory Theater in San Francisco.

How can a costume designer ensure that all the bases are covered for opening night? First and foremost, try to have the old standbys: time and money. "My one grand piece of wisdom for anyone undertaking the task of dressing actors for a play or musical is that you *must have* either time or money—and preferably both," says Ann Carnaby, who owns Tracy Theatre Originals. According to Carnaby, if a theatre has a severely limited budget, then the staff needs to schedule additional work hours to execute the costumes economically—"time to plan, time to shop for the best prices and time to explore less expensive alternatives."

By contrast, if there is little time to gather costumes, then a theatre should expect to spend more money on its wardrobe. In this case Carnaby recommends that the production staff go to a vendor whom they know and like, or to one known for its quality and reliability, rather than spending valuable time shopping around for a lower price from an unknown source.

Also critical to the success of costuming a production is effective communication. Cindy Catanese, owner of Disguises Costumes in Lakewood, Colo., recommends that designers clearly understand what the director wants from day one. "Ask questions, repeat things, draw pictures," she says. "Do everything you can do to make sure that you're on the same page as the director." It's critical that the designer study the script and create a costume plot, listing what's required for the production and blending all of the costumes together in a palette so that certain costumes don't overpower others—unless they're supposed to.

"You have to know the character before you costume him or her," says Schenz. "For example, is he or she a brazen personality or a milquetoast?" Beyond creating or renting a costume, a designer's job is to enhance each character, adds Schenz.

(Photo courtesy of Tracy Theatre Originals, Hampton, New Hampshire)

Floor notes that talking to the individual actors is also a key part of her job as a costume designer. "Be really communicative with the actors so that they trust you to produce the right wardrobe for them," she says. In addition, Carnaby and Schenz insist upon taking actors' measurements with a measuring tape rather than relying on a verbal estimate. "People typically take inches off the waist and add inches to the chest," says Schenz. "It's human nature. You need to ensure that the costume will fit properly, so double-check everything first." After preparing the wardrobe for a specific production, Catanese hangs all of the garments side-by-side on a rack. "I look to make sure everything matches all of the measurements, that nothing stands out and the show has a good overall look." Then Catanese provides each actor with a list of assigned pieces. This keeps pieces from disappearing and speeds the return of wardrobe at the end of a production.

Even with beautiful costumes that fit and hang just right, actors will sometimes experience difficulties before they go onstage. Many last-minute costume crises revolve around rips, tears and misplaced items — "zippers failing, buttons popping, costumes falling off," says Schenz. Adds Catanese, "I've had costume coordinators tell me that they broke zippers or the whole crotch of a pair of pants came apart." Even worse: actors who become enamored of a wardrobe item, take it home, and forget to bring it back. Floor notes that pieces disappear more often in small, local community theatre productions, which have a greater chance of actors leaving the theatre with their costume. "Then during a performance I'll hear, 'Oh, I forgot my hat!'" laughs Floor. "I know somebody who had to make replacement hat at the last minute using a paper plate and some toilet paper."

Leslie Darling's experience of constantly sewing up the same actor's zipper during multiple presentations of "Grease" is not atypical. During a recent production of "The Wizard of Oz" at the Cincinnati Playhouse, Jonn Schenz recalls a panicked last-minute zipper malfunction: "We had 30 seconds to sew an entire zipper into a costume before a guy went on stage." With so little time, costumer Deb Girdler couldn't rush the pants over to a sewing machine, so she had to hand-stitch everything on the spot. Although Girdler worked quickly, she still went through four new zippers before finding one that worked—and not a moment too soon.

What if there's no time to stitch a new zipper into someone's wardrobe? "That's when you slip in a safety pin and pray that it doesn't pop open when the actor's onstage," says Schenz, warning that the pin should be removed as soon as possible. "Otherwise," adds Darling, "you'll eventually tear the fabric in the costume." For last-minute patch-ups, in addition to needles and an assortment of threads, Darling says that costumers should carry scissors and a variety of hooks, snaps and zippers.

Every costume designer has his or her own pet peeve. For Jonn Schenz, it's hats. "Everyone takes their hat off first and then throws their wardrobe on top of it," he says, grimacing. "Then they wonder why the top hats aren't prim and proper." Ladies hats, especially, are susceptible to being crushed. But if an actor must lay a costume down, designers caution them to be careful. Darling warns against resting a costume anywhere near a light bulb. "The costume might burn," she says. "It's happened twice that I know of."

Sometimes the staff at rental houses can only shake their heads at the bizarre nature of some emergency modifications made in the field. Every year Schenz Theatrical Supply rents out a lot of bunny costumes, and not just to the White House. To keep the bunnies cuddly, the two-piece costumes are generous in size, with the crotch deliberately falling well below the waist for a comfortable fit. Nevertheless, one year a customer returned a bunny costume after making a rather bizarre makeshift repair: "They had duct-taped the crotch," Schenz recalls, shaking his head.

Sometimes there's little that can be done to correct a costume malfunction. "During the run of a show, you're going to get stains on some things and bust out the knees on others," says Schenz. "There's only so much that can be done." Callie Floor notes that the best way to deal with emergencies it to do things properly from the get-go. "Hopefully I've left these people in good enough shape, and made good choices, so they won't have wardrobe crises," she says.

In fashioning a new piece of wardrobe, designers need to consider future rental value as well. Schenz says he pays attention to the interior of a garment as much as the exterior. Rental costumes require a lifespan of 20 to 25 years to recoup the money put into their design and construction. "The price of a rental includes cleaning, alterations, depreciation, and packing and shipping if needed," says Schenz. "Therefore the garment must be made like cast iron. The last thing a performer needs to worry about when he gets onstage is his costume, so you darn well better make it right to start with."

Readying a show, and anticipating the emergencies that might occur, keep costume designers on the move. "Once a show is up and running," says Schenz, "anything can happen. But it's forethought that can keep most emergencies from happening. Just think of the worst-case scenario and be prepared for it."

12 Critical Items to have in your Costume Emergency Tool Kit

Arthur and Liza Chadwick, craft shop supervisor and master draper, respectively, for the annual Colorado Shakespeare Festival in Boulder, Colo., help build your emergency kit for last-minute costume mishaps:

1. Double-sided tape—in case a hem falls down or a performer is showing too much cleavage.
2. Pins—safety and bobby types, good for fast fixes. Liza carries them and also fastens a bunch to her own clothes for quick access.
3. Pliers—two pair of small, needle-nose type, to fix broken links or grommets.
4. Flashlight—in case you need to fix an emergency backstage, in the dark. Should be small enough to hang around your neck and be held between your teeth when necessary.
5. Scissors—hang them on a string around your neck.

6. Shoelaces—to replace broken ones on performers' footwear. Also good for tying things.

7. Spool of tie line—multiple uses, and can double as shoelaces when required.

8. Leather thimble—has a metal pad in it for pushing needles through thick material.

9. Contact information for cast and crew—put on a small card to hang around your neck with your scissors.

10. Lighter—to melt the tips of shoelaces or shrink tubes.

11. Comb—for light adjustments to performers' wigs.

12. Minty gum or breath mints—for people who might need them.

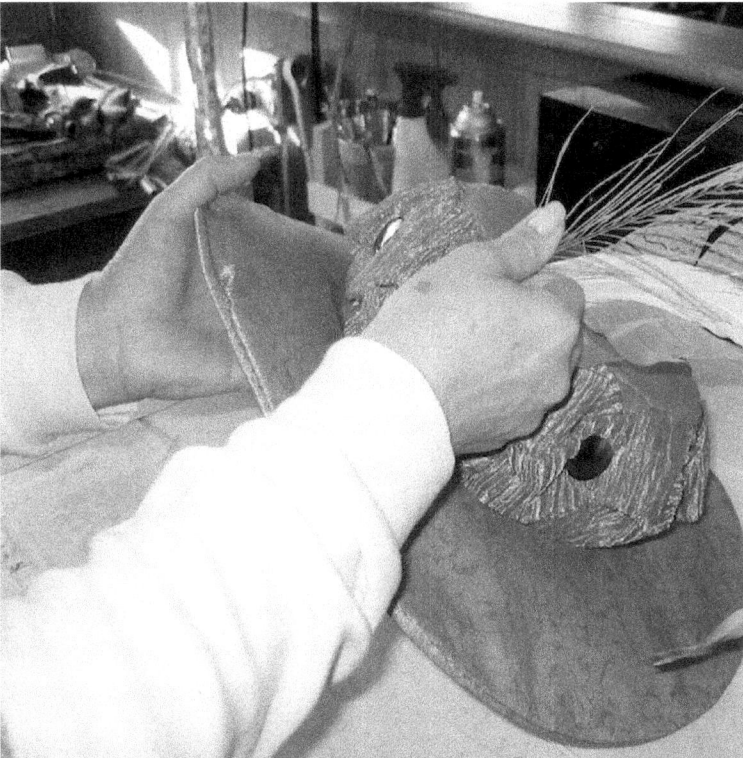

(Photo courtesy of Tracy Theatre Originals, Hampton, New Hampshire)

7 Secrets for Stopping Costume Emergencies in their Tracks

Leslie Darling, costume shop manager at Tracy Theatre Originals in Hampton, N.H., offers her tips for dealing with those pesky wardrobe problems:

1. Have someone ready who has a basic knowledge of sewing with a needle and thread.
2. Be prepared for the unexpected. If a costume malfunctions before curtain call, you'll need to fix it on the spot. There probably won't be time to use a sewing machine.
3. Then again, there might be time available. So if possible, having a sewing machine standing by as well.
4. Keep a small supply of basic items on hand, including scissors and a good variety of zippers, snaps, hooks, needles and threads in different colors.
5. Safety pins are useful if you need to fix something immediately, but they should never be left in the garment because they'll eventually rip the fabric.
6. Gaffer's tape is a no-no. (Believe it or not, Darling has had costumes come back with gaff tape holding them together). The same goes for duct tape.
7. Your most important tool is having someone on the crew who isn't going to panic about the problem and just fixes what's wrong.

7 things every costume designer wishes the director would do

Callie Floor of the American Conservatory Theater in San Francisco and Arthur and Liza Chadwick of the Colorado Shakespeare Festival offer their thoughts on how to make a show run smoothly:

1. Understand the resources available. Look at the kinds of projects that are being scheduled, and check to see if the theatre has the proper resources to put on that kind of show.

2. Communicate with your costume designer. At each step in the process of creating a wardrobe—determining a color palette, preparing sketches, reviewing fabric swatches—you make decisions that obligate more of your production money, so choose carefully.

3. Likewise, the costume designer should be communicating with you regularly about how the wardrobe is progressing.

4. Once you've assembled a team of professionals to dress your production, trust them to do their jobs. Don't micromanage or second-guess their efforts.

5. Be concerned with the big picture rather than the intricacies of costume design. Instead of requesting that a pair of pants be shortened, check to see if the costume is presenting the image you want. Let the costume designer do the rest.

6. Provide the costume designer with notes during the rehearsal process. Now that you've seen the wardrobe onstage, are there small changes that you'd like made to them?

7. Don't make last-minute changes to the wardrobe. One small change can have a ripple effect on the entire cast and crew.

Automated Rigging Systems:
Safe, reliable solutions for all of your staging and engineering needs

Mounted above and around your stage is an assortment of grids, bars, pulleys and winches—all the rigging tools to making your productions come alive. Is your crew pulling and pushing by hand, or is your rigging system computer-controlled with electronic gear? Many theatres have chosen to automate, while some prefer to stick with traditional methods. If you're considering a switch, there's a lot more at stake than simple convenience.

The traditional approach, known as manual counterweight rigging, utilizes an arbor (rack) loaded with counterweights to balance whatever curtains, lights or scenery hang from a pipe batten (bar). (Some theatres use sandbags instead of weights.) Loading and moving the system requires old-fashioned elbow grease on the part of the crew. By contrast, automated rigging setups feature electric motors and range from simple push-button, up-and-down winches to custom-designed creations that mechanize everything from fire curtains to fly spaces.

To Convert or Not to Convert

Although snazzy automated rigging might provide smoother, safer command of moving objects in your theatre, not every theatre has rushed to modernize its systems. As always, cost is a determining factor.

Some theatres choose to automate in a limited fashion and wait until later to add more equipment. Rigging specialist J.R. Clancy, Inc., helped outfit the new Arts Center in Mesa, Ariz., which features four theatres seating 1,600, 550, 200 and 99 patrons, respectively. For now, only the fire curtains and the acoustic reflector at the front of the proscenium in the largest theatre are automated. "The decision was primarily driven by cost and the need for flexibility in the fly towers," says Mike McMackin, principal with Auerbach Pollock Friedlander in San Francisco, who served as consultant on the project. If the Center decides to automate more of its features, "there's plenty of power available for future expansion," he adds.

Installing a motorized rigging setup can also result in significant savings to a theatre's bottom line, says Karl Ruling, technical standards manager for the Entertainment Services and Technology Association, a nonprofit trade organization in New York, N.Y. Ruling notes that automation can help alleviate high-budget items like labor, insurance premiums and liability payments to employees injured on the job. "Automated systems are almost always aimed at getting rid of the job of loading and unloading arbors, so that physically taxing job is eliminated," he explains. "And the risk of runaway arbors is eliminated as well."

In addition, automated systems can significantly reduce load-in time and allow productions to run complicated scene shifts with smaller crews.

What Can Be Automated?

Depending on your budget, anything in your theatre can be automated. "Any and all of the theatrical rigging battens, including electrics and orchestra shell ceiling battens, can be motorized and controlled by an automated system," says Ted Paget, regional sales manager for Vortek in Victor, N.Y. "This includes hoisting equipment—as well as orchestra pit lifts—furnished by other manufacturers."

Dan Culhane of equipment vendor SECOA, Inc., in Champlin, Minn., recommends that electrics/lighting line sets be automated. "They're also the most economical to convert from manual operation to a counterweight assist winch," he explains. Culhane notes that a simple computer control for preset elevations would be useful, as the electrics are frequently lowered to the deck for gel and gobo changes during the run of a show. Rather than having to raise the electrics by hand, an automated system can whisk the equipment back to its previous position at the touch of a button.

Counterweight assist winches, part of an automated rigging package. *(Photo courtesy of SECOA Inc.)*

Thinking about converting

If you're looking at converting, it's time to create a checklist of items to consider. First of all, will your building support the type of automation you'd like to install? If your stage has modern counterweight rigging, automating it should be a relatively painless process, says Paget. "But if your stage still has hemp-and-sandbag rigging—or, worse yet, dead-hung (fixed) rigging—it will need a thorough structural analysis."

According to Culhane, adding new hoists—especially high-speed ones—can increase loads as much as 180 percent over the weight of the item being lifted. To run a large automated system, "it's not unusual to need 100 amps or more of dedicated power," he says. Because older buildings generally aren't capable of supporting this type of power requirement, Culhane notes, theatre owners might be forced to green-light major electrical upgrades.

Next, where will you mount the rigging motors, and how will technicians access them when they need servicing? "Usually if the stage has counterweight or hemp-and-sandbag rigging there will be at least one service platform and a set of head beams," says Paget. If this is the case, the contractor can determine whether to install the mechanism vertically on one or more walls or horizontally from the ceiling or existing rigging grid.

To sort all this out, your best bet is to hire a consultant to guide you. "In the long run," says Culhane, "a theatre consultant will save you money." Ruling recommends that, if possible, you first contact the vendor that installed your existing rigging system.

Paget adds that talking to a vendor's sales manager can also help. "Some of us can develop initial layout drawings to assist with identifying building-related concerns—pipes, conduits and other items that might conflict with the new rigging—and prepare a good preliminary estimate of rigging weight loads, electrical requirements and costs," he says.

Budget Considerations

Costs can vary widely depending on the type of system being installed. Are you automating an existing system, or do you want to create a customized setup? How sophisticated is the new system?

Does it coordinate multiple hoists at various speeds? If so, what are the speeds and capacities of the hoists?

Paget recommends that theatre managers mull over possible budget-busters like the complexity of any required demolition, structural or electrical modifications or upgrades, and access to the stage from load-in points, to name a few. "Each project should have a preliminary budget in order to determine how much funding to seek," he adds. As with any renovation project, the budget should allow for a reasonable contingency.

Culhane offers the following price comparison to theatres looking at a new system: "Installing a manual counterweight line set costs between $6,000 and $7,000 each," he says. "A counterweight assist with simple up, down and emergency-stop controls will cost $15,000. Add a single computer control with programmable elevation settings and that will cost an additional $5,000." A complete packaged hoist system can cost between $25,000 and $30,000 per winch to install.

Down time

Keep in mind that your theatre will undergo some down time as you convert your rigging system. "A good installation crew can convert one to two manual counterweight sets a day to a counterweight assist hoisting system," says Culhane. "A packaged hoist system may take an installation crew approximately two days per set to remove the existing equipment and install the new system."

Wheaton Warrenville South High School in Wheaton, Ill., selected Vortek to automate the rigging system in its theatre. The contractor took about eight weeks to complete the project. "We planned our schedule around it," recalls Phil Britton, assistant principal for fine and performing arts and activities, "during a time when very little was occurring in our auditorium."

There are, of course, other considerations that have nothing to do with installation of the rigging. Make sure you include blocks of time in your schedule for the electrical contractor, says Paget:

"The electrician must furnish power to the rigging system, as well as low-voltage conduit and control wire."

Safety Considerations

As with any new system, safety is a key consideration. Paget notes that improvements in the mechanical "drive through" load brake on packaged hoists—which regulates downward movement—reduce the likelihood of an emergency stop. "Sudden stops can shake the pipe batten and could cause all or part of the load to fall," he explains. This type of accident can affect the support structure of the theatre itself. This is a major concern on the stages of existing theatres, adds Paget, because they weren't designed to withstand quick decelerations of moving loads.

Automation doesn't need to be complex. Paget points to Vortek's packaged hoist rigging as an example of a product that can be used easily by novice operators. Rather than repeatedly loading and unloading counterweight arbors to balance each batten, the crew uses show loads instead. A computer program then controls the batten by adjusting operating weights for the hoist when it's raising or lowering a load.

At Wheaton Warrenville South High School, "we wanted to convert our system for safety reasons and for ease of use," says Assistant Principal Britton. The software controlling the rigging is protected with passwords to lock out anyone who isn't authorized to use the system.

Training

Because an automated rigging system can be more complicated to operate than a traditional manual counterweight system, training requirements vary. "Some controls are little more than a couple of buttons," says Ruling. "Some have buttons and also levers for proportional speed control. Some are as complicated as lighting control desks—perhaps more so."

"It is always important for users to become familiar with the users manual," says Paget, "but nothing can substitute for thorough training provided by a knowledgeable technician." Vortek, for example, dispatches field service technicians to train clients in their new systems.

Whatever level of automated rigging you decide to implement, remember that you have a variety of choices from simple to incredibly intricate. "The ultimate in automated rigging today is what we're doing with Cirque du Soleil's permanent venues," says Mike McMackin. Cirque shows feature multiple performers suspended in midair, along with colorful, fast-moving drops and props. The computer controls feature bright, colorful 3-D touch screens. "We push the envelope in terms of what can be done in terms of rigging, automation, and invention of new systems," says McMackin.

Should you automate? Here are some things to consider:

What capabilities do you need in an automated system?

Will the existing infrastructure of your theatre support the type of system you'd like to install?

Should you purchase a rigging package, or have a contractor custom-design a system for you?

What's your budget? Costs for automated systems vary greatly depending on how many features you want.

Does your production schedule allow for the down time required to install a new system?

Will an automated system improve the quality of your productions for both the audience and the crew?

About the Author

Allan T. Duffin is a freelance writer and television/multimedia producer. He writes books and Internet, magazine, and newspaper articles. For television he has written, produced, co-produced, and developed programs for the History and Discovery networks. Allan is a veteran of the U.S. Air Force. Visit his website at www.aduffin.com.

Books by Allan T. Duffin, available at Amazon.com

Catch the Sky: The Adventures and Misadventures of a Police Helicopter Pilot
Duffin Creative

History in Blue: 160 Years of Women Police, Sheriffs, Detectives, and State Troopers
Kaplan Publishing/Simon & Schuster

The "12 O'Clock High" Logbook: The Unofficial History of the Novel, Motion Picture, and Television Series
BearManor Media

Tow Truck Kings: Secrets of the Towing & Recovery Business
Available from Amazon.com

Tow Truck Kings 2: More Secrets of the Towing & Recovery Business
Available from Amazon.com

TheatreBook: A Compact Guide to Running Your Theatre
Available from Amazon.com